Skills for Success
for your
third grader

A+ Student

Written by
Glenda Frasier

Illustrations by
Marilee Harrald-Pilz

Cover Photography by Anthony Nex of Anthony Nex Photography

Photo Credits: © 1997 Comstock, Inc.: pages 3, 12, 16, 31, 38, 43, 53, 56, 57, 59, 60, 63, 65

FS-23004 Skills for Success for Your Third Grader
All rights reserved—Printed in the U. S. A. Copyright © 1997 Frank Schaffer Publications, Inc.

Table of Contents

The Thrilling Third Grader!

WHAT Are THIRD Graders Like?

Parents wear many hats every day. Each one is equally important, but sometimes parents are nervous about wearing the hat of "teacher" for their child. The truth is that all day every day the invisible "teacher hat" is perched on your head, perhaps even on top of another hat you may be wearing at the moment! The joy of parenting comes with making the most of every opportunity to be your child's "teacher."

Parents can be nervous about performing the role of teacher because they are not sure what expectations or goals are realistic for their child at each level. This book is aimed at helping you understand, appreciate, and accentuate the learning that your child is ready to experience.

You were and still are your child's first and most important teacher. By becoming familiar with the skills a third grader needs, you can be more efficient and effective as you continue in that role.

* They are **honest** both in compliments and complaints. They express opinions without hesitation.

* They are **imaginative**. Give them a box of odds 'n' ends and watch the creations develop.

* They are **remarkable**. Their capacity to live and learn and love is bottomless.

* They are **determined**. Involve them in a project or event and watch the commitment emerge!

* They are **gracious** with others and seek many friendships with people of all ages.

* They are **risk takers**. They like to be the leaders and investigate new horizons.

* They are **anxious** to be the best they can be and need constant encouragement.

* They are **discoverers**. Problem solving becomes an adventure to be conquered.

* They are **exuberant**. Their curiosity propels them into learning with vitality.

* They are **ready** to learn and grow with your direction and the ideas in this book.

The Keys to Using This Book

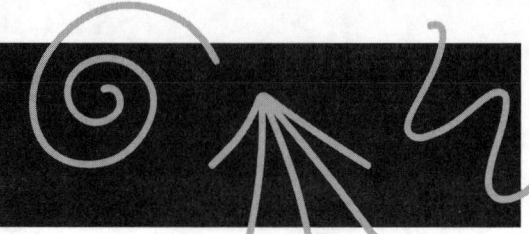

Be a Learner

Be ready to tell your child that you don't know something. A question from your child indicates interest in the topic, but you don't need to feel embarrassed if you don't know the answer. The important step is to help them look for an answer.

Teach to the Moment

Remember that the best time to teach anything is the moment your child has expressed curiosity about it. If your child asks a question about the phases of the moon, try to provide information, look it up with him or her in a science book or encyclopedia, and watch the sky. If you have access to the Internet or a computer with a multimedia reference tool, use that to gain instant facts to share.

Teach Academic Skills

The first section of this book provides a guide for you full of activities that center around the topics third graders study in school. Use it to help your child better understand a topic that is being taught and to enhance what your child is learning at school. Use it as background information to provide ideas for you to use when interacting with your child.

Teach Social Skills

The next section centers around social skills. Even the most intelligent child will be less successful in school without good personal skills. These interpersonal skills are critical for positive relationships to develop and for your child to feel worthwhile. Use this section to provide an approach to a problem or an opening to discuss a topic. With prior discussion about these vital skills, your child will have strategies to deal with concerns when they appear.

Promote Home and School Cooperation

The next section of this book gives you practical ideas for how to navigate home and school interaction on a daily basis. There are suggestions for organizing, communicating with the educational community, conferencing with teachers, and getting involved at school.

Give Praise

Included in the book are reward items. Use these to show your child that you are proud of his or her efforts. Children respond to positive reinforcement. Teachers know that the more specific the praise, the better. "Good job!" is great to hear, but more repeat performances come from phrases such as "You wrote your story so neatly that it is easy for me to read. That shows me you are proud of it, too!"

Give Practice

The final section consists of skill pages for your child. Use them to check on your child's understanding of a skill. Use them to provide individual practice for a skill. Use them to provide a chance for your child to demonstrate progress! If your child has difficulty, you may want to repeat an activity or choose a new approach to helping him or her master that skill.

Reading Skills Third Graders Need

PHONICS, WORD ANALYSIS, AND VOCABULARY

* Recognize and use consonant blends at the beginning of words (Ex: *br-, pl-, scr-, st-*)

* Recognize and use consonant blends at the end of words (Ex: *-nt, -ld*)

* Recognize and use consonant digraphs [two letters that make one sound] at the beginning and end of words (Ex: *th, ch, sh*)

* Recognize and use long and short vowels in words

* Recognize that two vowels together may make a special sound of their own (Ex: *oy* in *boy*; *ou* in *pout*; *au* in *haul*; *ew* in *new*)

* Recognize and use endings on words, such as *-ed, -s, -es, -ing, -er, -est*

* Understand that words are made of parts, or beats, called syllables and that each syllable has at least one vowel (Ex: *child*, one syllable; *par ent*, two syllables)

* Identify contractions and the words they are made of (Ex: *can't–can not, I'm–I am*)

* Understand possessives, such as *Susie's bicycle* or *the boys' bats*

* Recognize rhyming words

* Recognize spelling patterns in words, such as *coat, poach, throat*

* Recognize compound words

* Understand synonyms [words that mean about the same] (Ex: *grin* and *smile*)

* Understand antonyms [words that mean the opposite] (Ex: *happy* and *sad*)

* Understand homophones [words that sound alike but have different meanings and spellings] (Ex: *pear* and *pair*)

* Understand that some words that look alike may have different meanings, such as *bank* (land along a water's edge) and *bank* (a place where money is kept)

COMPREHENSION

* Understand that a paragraph has a main idea and supporting details

* Recall details from text

* Predict what will happen next

* Sequence the events in the story

* Summarize the main points in a story

* Develop an ability to explain cause and effect

* Draw logical conclusions from their reading

* Know the difference between fact and opinion

* Know the difference between fiction and nonfiction

* Tell the meaning of common expressions

* Read and follow directions

* Use drawings, maps, and charts that accompany the text to help understand it

* Draw pictures or diagrams to explain the text

VENTURING THROUGH VOWEL LAND!

> Vowels are a, e, i, o, u and sometimes y. Vowels make a variety of sounds in words.

If you pretend that a word is like a jelly sandwich, the consonants are the bread and the vowels are the jelly. The consonants make the framework of the word, and the vowels give the word a special "flavor" or uniqueness that lets us discriminate that word from other words.

For example, look at these frames: a) s__d b) m__n. The first word could be sad, sod, said, seed, or sued. The second word could be man, men, main, mean, or moon. We don't know for sure until we add the vowels.

Third graders need to advance beyond short and long vowels and gain competency recognizing other vowel sounds, such as digraphs (school, book, yawn) diphthongs (out, joy, new) r-controlled vowels (her, stare, word), and the schwa sound (about, the, other).

Because vowels can make so many different sounds, some children have difficulty with them. Help your child if you see specific vowel sounds that are problematic.

A great way to practice vowels with your child is to point out tricky combinations as you read together. When the word "terror" appears, you can mention the "r-controlled" vowels that are found in that word. Whenever "Bossy R" follows a vowel, it changes the sound the vowel makes. The repetition your child sees and hears in literature will help cement the phonics rules that are taught at school.

VOWEL TIC-TAC-TOE

Each player selects a vowel sound to practice, for example ou and ea. (You may want to check with your child's teacher on specific sounds to work with.) The game is played just like tic-tac-toe except players write words with their corresponding vowel sound, rather than X's or O's.

The winner in this game is the ou player who wrote three ou words in a row.

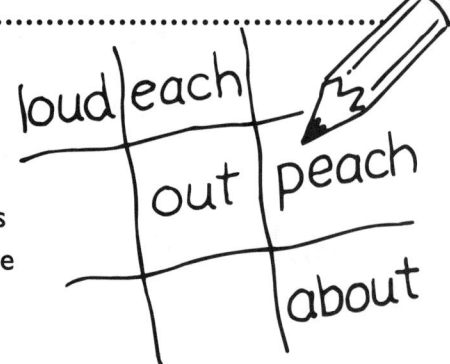

VOWEL BOWLING

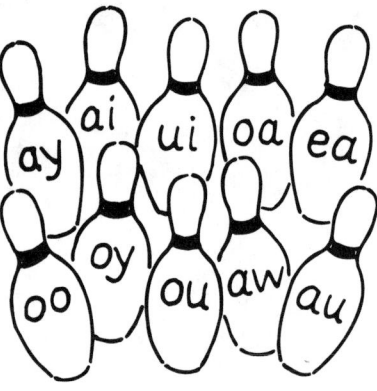

For this activity you need a set of plastic bowling pins and a ball. (These are available at discount stores in the toy department or sometimes at yard sales.) Use a permanent marker to write vowel letters or combinations on each pin. Set them up and join your child in a game of bowling. For every pin knocked down, the player must give a word with that vowel sound in it. For every word that is correct, a point is awarded. The winner is the bowler with the most points at the end of the ten rolls.

COMPOUND HANG-UPS

This is a great outdoor activity for spelling or vocabulary practice. Using a dark marker, write words that could be part of a compound word on the flat side of a springtype clothespin. Give your child some strips of plain paper and a marker.

Direct your child to match up two clothespins to make a compound word. Have your child write the compound word on a strip of paper and tell you a sentence with the word in it. (That's a good check to see if it is a real word that makes sense.)

Hang the strips on the clothesline with the two matching clothespins. See if you can fill up the whole clothesline. If you don't have a clothesline or it is too high for your child, just tie a string between two chairs. This now becomes a great indoor activity!

> Compounds are two words put together to make a new word with a new meaning. Some are written as one word like "grandmother" and some are written as two words like " ice cream."

anyone	cowboy
without	maybe
Sunday	scarecrow
tonight	bulldog
birthday	sunset
pigpen	everywhere
upon	railroad
somebody	crosswalk
beehive	footprint
starfish	sunburn
inside	herself
grandson	newspaper
bedroom	cobweb
horsefly	baseball
snowball	touchdown
daydream	earring
toothpick	

A FUN VARIATION

Cut paper socks from light colored paper or if you have some old white socks that are headed for the rag bag, use them! Using a black marker, write each part of the compound word on its own sock. Toss them into a basket and let your child search for the matches! Hang them on the line with one clothespin.

Use words from your child's lessons or try some of these listed on the left.

COMPOUND QUESTIONS

Write and illustrate compound word questions.

Did you ever see a horse fly?

Did you ever see a star fish?

CONTRACTIONS

* As you read with your child, point out contractions in the stories. Reread the sentence substituting the two words for the contraction. Ask how the sentences are different. Is one way better than the other? Do the sentences mean the same thing?

* Use a red marker to circle contractions you find in the newspaper.

Contractions are shortened words that are made by combining words, leaving out one or more letters, and putting an apostrophe in their place.
Example: is + not = isn't

* Write contractions like these on a piece of paper. Have your child identify the two words that make up each contraction.

he'll	wasn't	I've	she'll
wouldn't	you've	it's	didn't
could've	that's	don't	we're
who's	won't	they're	I'd
needn't	I'm	you'd	can't

ANTONYMS

A mastery of antonyms helps your child read and write better. It increases the listening and speaking vocabulary which in turn increases comprehension. To practice antonyms try these games:

Antonym Checkers—Using a regular checkerboard, either write one word on each square or write the word on self-sticking notes and lay them on the squares.

The object of the game is to pronounce the word and give an "opposite" every time your checker lands on that square.

Antonym Hide and Seek—Write each of the antonyms listed below on separate cards. Hide half of each antonym pair in a specified area, like the living room or the backyard. Give your child the other set of cards. The object is for your

Antonyms are words that mean the opposite.
Example: stop-go

child to find the hidden words and match the opposites.

day-night	black-white	sad-happy	sun-moon
catch-throw	clean-dirty	open-shut	smile-frown
up-down	silly-serious	on-off	noisy-quiet
pull-push	straight-crooked	good-bad	first-last
part-whole	shiny-dull	front-back	never-always
walk-run	broken-repaired	sit-stand	win-lose
play-work	light-heavy	hard-soft	sink-float

SEARCH for meaning!

Scan
Examine
Ask
Read
Check
Help!

Celebrate your learning!

SEARCH!

Help your child get the most out of every reading activity. No matter what kind of text needs to be read the SEARCH method will help your child get the meaning! It gets the reader's mind set on what will be read.

Teach your child to do these steps:

SCAN—Look over the information from start to finish. Take a look at the pictures and predict what is going to happen.

EXAMINE—Read the bold print, questions along the side, and paragraph or chapter headings. Think about the way the book or article is put together.

ASK—Ask questions about what you saw. How does it fit together? Why did the author choose that title? How do the pictures fit with the story? Ask yourself the questions or ask a reading partner. Jot them down if you like.

READ—Now you are ready to read the text word for word. Watch punctuation and sentence structure.

CHECK—Check yourself on your reading. See if you can answer the questions you asked in the beginning. Did you understand what you read? Draw a picture of what you read, make a chart about the article, or write a few sentences about the story.

HELP—Get help if you didn't understand what you read. Ask an adult, look up the topic in another book or encyclopedia, or talk about it with a friend.

Once you understand, **celebrate** your learning.

Make several copies of this bookmark for your child to use while reading.

THAT'S THE MAIN IDEA!

Understanding the main idea of a paragraph lets your child get the most meaning out of reading. It is a difficult skill and requires lots of practice. Giving your child a visual picture of the main idea will help make it clearer. Many children and adults learn better by hooking a picture to a skill. Try this main idea tree activity with your child.

Draw and label the tree frame as shown below. (If you draw it on a chalkboard or whiteboard, you can reuse the frame.) When your child finishes reading a paragraph, fill in the branches of the tree with details. Then discuss and write the main idea that unifies the different details.

It is not necessary to do this process with every paragraph. Select an important lesson and do one or two paragraphs periodically for practice.

The main idea is the focus of a paragraph. All or most of the information in the paragraph relates to the main idea.

When your child has trouble understanding a passage, return to this picture. Visualizing this graphic will help your child organize and remember information.

PUT IT IN ORDER!

> Sequencing is recalling the order of events. It may take different forms including retelling what happened in a story or listing steps in directions.

✳ Give your child three directions to do. For example: *Pick up the book. Turn around three times. Sit down on the couch.* See if your child can remember and complete all three in order. Now let your child test you! Purposely make a mistake and let your child correct you. As the skill level increases, add more steps to remember.

✳ Read a story with your child and talk about what happened first, next, and last. If this is difficult, reread that part of the story. Show your child that reviewing and revisiting the text is a great study skill. You can also do this when reading a chapter book to your child. Review the events from the previously read chapter to set the stage for what you will read next.

✳ Draw a ladder like the one shown here or ask your child to draw one. Label the bottom rung the beginning of the story and the top rung the ending. Together discuss and write a sentence, phrase, or word that describes the beginning of the story. On each step upward, write a sentence, phrase, or word that tells what happened next. Be sure your child understands the idea that every story or article has a beginning, middle, and end. Each part should be full of details to explain what is happening. Encourage your child to recall as many details as possible from the story.

The Talking Eggs

Ending

Rose and her mom were chased into the forest by wasps and wolves. Blanche lived happily ever after.

Rose made fun of the woman and didn't do what she said. She took the wrong eggs.

Blanche's sister, Rose, tried to get eggs from the woman.

Blanche did what the woman said and was rewarded with magic eggs.

The woman had strange things but was nice to Blanche.

Blanche met an old woman while fetching water.

Blanches's mom and sister were mean to her.

Beginning

FACT OR OPINION

Third graders need to begin to recognize the difference between what is a fact and what is someone's opinion. This is not only an important reading skill, but an important life skill as well. Use the statements in the gray box on this page to help your child recognize the difference between fact and opinion.

Flash Card Facts—Give your child a flash card that says "fact" on one side and "opinion" on the other.

Discuss the difference. Then read a statement from this page and let your child show you the correct label. For fun, the flash card could be glued to a dowel or stick for your child to hold.

Fruity Facts—Place a small bowl of green and red grapes in front of your child. Label the green bowl "fact" and the red bowl "opinion." When you say a statement, have your child point to fact or opinion. If the answer is correct, your child gets to eat a grape of that color. If the answer is incorrect, try again! Take turns being the host and the eater. You can use any snack your child enjoys, just be sure you have two bowls of different items.

A fact is a true statement that can be proven. An opinion is someone's belief.

Noticing Newspapers—As you read the newspaper, cut out advertisements that would interest your child. Share these some evening and discuss whether they express facts or opinions. You can adapt this idea to reading a cereal box and study it at breakfast time. Your child will become a wiser consumer!

Pizza Predictions—Begin with two paper plates or cut two 10" circles from paper or cardboard. Divide the circles into six slices and write one of the statements from the gray box on each slice. You can also make up some of your own. Scramble the pieces and let your child put together a "fact" pizza and an "opinion" pizza.

1. The earth is round.
2. Blue is most people's favorite color.
3. Plants have roots.
4. There are twelve eggs in a dozen.
5. Pepperoni pizza tastes best.
6. A black car runs better than others.
7. Girls are smarter than boys.
8. Six times three equals eighteen.
9. An airplane is faster than a train.
10. My mother's perfume smells good.
11. The council should vote yes.
12. There are seven days in a week.

Wonderful Books for Third Graders to Explore

These books may be found at your school or public library. They would make perfect gifts for any occasion. Check your local bookstore. You will enjoy these, too!

Picture Books

Annie and the Old One by Miska Miles (Little, Brown, 1971)

Cloudy with a Chance of Meatballs by Judith Barrett (Macmillan, 1982)

Family Pictures/Cuadros de familia by Carmen Lomas Garza (Children's Book Press, 1990)

Grandfather Tang's Story by Ann Tompert (Crown, 1990)

Hershel and the Hanukkah Goblins by Eric A. Kimmel (Holiday, 1989)

The Great Kapok Tree by Lynne Cherry (Harcourt Brace Jovanovich, 1990)

Miss Rumphius by Barbara Cooney (Viking, 1982)

Chapter Books

Freckle Juice by Judy Blume (Macmillan, 1971)

How to Eat Fried Worms by Thomas Rockwell (Watts, 1973)

Mr. Popper's Penguins by Richard & Florence Atwater (Little, Brown, 1938)

Sarah, Plain and Tall by Patricia MacLachlan (Harper & Row, 1985)

Sideways Stories From Wayside School by Louis Sachar (Random House, 1990)

The Twenty-One Balloons by William Pene du Bois (Viking, 1947)

. . . and thousands more!

Folklore

Her Stories: African American Folktales, Fairy Tales, and True Tales by Virginia Hamilton (Scholastic, 1995)

The Adventures of Robin Hood by Marcia Williams (Candlewick, 1995)

The Stinky Cheese Man and Other Fairly Stupid Tales by Jon Scieszka (Viking, 1992)

Poetry

Night on Neighborhood Street by Eloise Greenfield (Dial, 1991)

Something Big Has Been Here by Jack Prelutsky (Greenwillow, 1990)

Where the Sidewalk Ends by Shel Silverstein (Harper & Row, 1974)

These authors have written many books that Third Graders will enjoy:

Picture Books

Harry Allard	Paul Goble
Mitsumasa Anno	William Steig
Molly Bang	Chris Van Allsburg
Jan Brett	Judith Viorst
Carol Carrick	Jane Yolen
Joanna Cole	

Informational Books

Aliki
George Ancona
Franklyn Branley
Jean Fritz
Gail Gibbons
Jill Krementz
Ellen Levine
Mike Venezia
Kate Waters

Chapter Books

Beverly Cleary
Roald Dahl
Mary Pope Osborne
Barbara Park
Daniel M. Pinkwater
Dick King-Smith
Donald Sobol

Language Arts Skills Third Graders Need

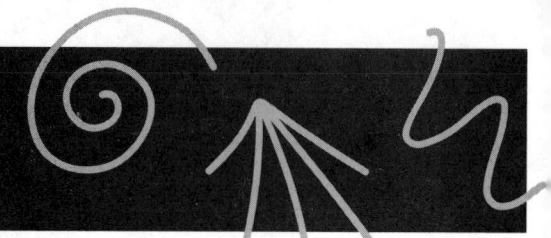

WRITING

* Understand what makes a complete sentence

* Understand that a paragraph is made of a main idea sentence and supporting sentences

* Create stories with a beginning, middle, and end

* Use descriptive words to create a picture for the reader

* Include details about setting, theme, plot, and characters in the writing

* Include who, what, where, when, why, and how in a composition

* Write a report on a nonfiction topic

* Write a friendly letter

* Address an envelope

* Create poetry

* Follow a step-by-step process for writing

* Understand that each piece of writing may have a specific audience

* Edit writing that is for others to read

* Write legibly

* Capitalize words correctly

* Use punctuation correctly

* See themselves as writers

* Enjoy sharing their writing with others in a variety of ways

SPELLING

* Spell basic sight words

* Understand that the same sound may have a variety of spellings

* Apply basic spelling rules

* Follow a step-by-step process to learn to spell new words

* Use phonics and spelling skills to locate words in a dictionary or spell checker

GRAMMAR

* Recognize that nouns are names of people, places, and things

* Recognize that proper nouns are the names of special people, places, or things and need to be capitalized

* Recognize action words as verbs

* Recognize adjectives as words that describe

* Understand that a sentence has a subject and a predicate

PENMANSHIP

* Write neatly using manuscript alphabet (printing)

* Form letters correctly

* Practice cursive writing

THE WRITING PROCESS

Many teachers show students a five-step process for writing. While the writing process may vary, these are the primary steps to follow.

Prewriting

* Brainstorm ideas
* Ask questions
* Research the topic
* Talk about it with others
* Share ideas
* Make a list of words you may need
* Jot down notes
* Draw a picture
* Make a mind web to categorize the ideas

Draft writing

* Focus on the ideas you want to include
* Write phrases, sentences, and paragraphs
* Stress content and ideas not structure at this point

Talk and Share

* Read it to a partner or teacher
* Discuss changes
* Look for new ways to write something
* Check for audience understanding
* Confer with others

Edit

* Revise sentences
* Elaborate on details
* Enhance words you chose
* Connect the ideas
* Proofread for spelling, structure, grammar, punctuation, and capital letters

Publish

* Rewrite using the revised draft
* Create a final draft
* Share it with a group or the class
* Make a book
* Display it on a bulletin board
* Tape record or videotape it

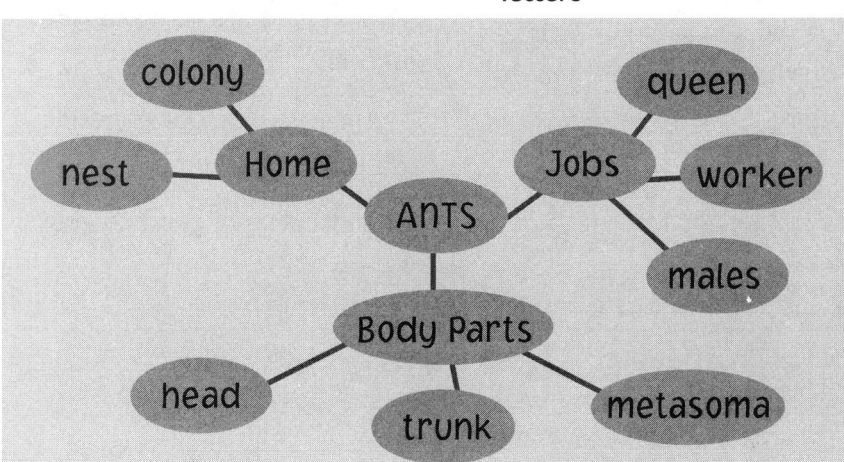

A mind web gives the learner a visual way to think about the topic. It can be simple or very elaborate, but its purpose is to give structure to the writing.

USING COMPLETE SENTENCES

Before third graders can write complete sentences, they must be able to speak in complete sentences. Insist that your child use complete sentences in discussions and speak to them in complete sentences. There will certainly be times in family conversation when complete sentences or answers are not feasible. Whenever possible, however, model correct language because that is the best way to teach it. Do not criticize your child's language, just repeat it correctly and ask him or her to say it again.

The next step is to recognize sentence fragments and complete sentences. Write or say some partial sentences and see if your child can identify the error. If this is difficult, draw a diagram and let your child fill in the parts. Third graders can usually label the subject (whom or what the sentence is about), predicate (what the subject is doing), and adjectives (words that describe).

Example: Silly frogs eat peanut butter.

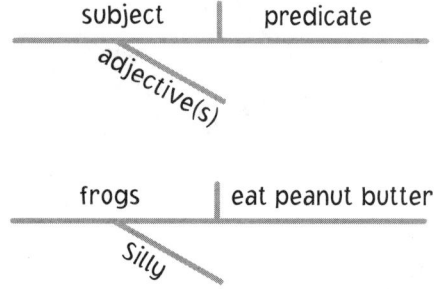

✳ For a hands-on activity, cut out a red and a blue paper strip. Write the subject of the sentence on the red one, and the predicate on the blue. If there is nothing to write on one strip, then the sentence is not complete.

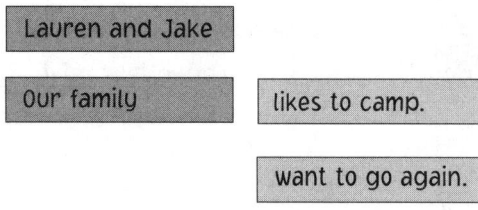

TYPES OF SENTENCES

Third graders are learning that there are different types of sentences.

✳ Telling sentence (statement)

✳ Asking sentence (question)

✳ Exciting sentence (exclamation)

As you ride in the car or wait in line at the grocery store, tell your child a sentence. Ask what kind of sentence it is and what punctuation should go at the end.

✳ Telling sentence—period

✳ Asking sentence—question mark

✳ Exciting sentence—exclamation point

While reading with your child, point out the variety of sentences that are found in the story. Ask your child to describe what kind of sentence each one is. Point out the punctuation that is used.

Use sentences like these to demonstrate the difference punctuation makes:

Anna, you are going to ride with me.

Anna, you are going to ride with me?

Anna, you *are* going to ride with me!

WRITE RIGHT!

Incorporate writing into every aspect of your child's day to demonstrate the importance of the skill. Your child will begin to realize that written communication is vital to becoming a literate adult. Make the projects fun.

Personalized Stationery—Create personalized stationery for your child to write notes and letters on. Choose a rubber stamp that exemplifies a hobby or interest of your child. Stamp several pieces of plain or lined paper with the design. Stamp plain envelopes with the same design to create matching sets. Tie the sheets together with a bright ribbon or lay them in a box covered with wallpaper scraps or self-adhesive paper. Do the same with a rubber stamp that represents your interests. Write notes to your child on the stationery and ask questions that your child will have to answer in a written response.

Photo Stationery—For a variation on the personalized stationery idea, use a small photo such as your child's school picture. If you attach it to a white sheet of paper and make a copy, your child's photo will appear at the top of every letter he or she writes. Grandparents love to receive Photo Stationery from their grandchildren. The entire family can get involved by using a family photo. Then each member of the family could add a paragraph before the letter is sent to a favorite relative or friend.

Mailboxes—Create a "mailbox" for each member of the family using letter files or cereal boxes with the side cut out. "Mail" letters and notes to all members of the family.

Lunch Box Notes—Stick a friendly note in your child's lunch box. Remind your child of something fun the family is doing that evening.

Refrigerator Memos—If your child gets home before you do in the evening, you could leave a note on the refrigerator telling about a special snack. When time allows, give clues to the location of the snack instead of just telling your child where it is.

Comic Writer—Have your child cut comic strips out of the newspaper and cut off or black out the conversation balloons that show what the characters are saying. Create your own conversation according to the pictures and actions you see in the comic strip.

No Talking!—Set aside a period of time such as an afternoon for no talking. Challenge everyone in the family to communicate only through written notes.

EDITING STRATEGIES

Third graders understand that writing has different purposes and different audiences. Sometimes a writer is composing just for himself. That is often a rough draft or just notes. Sometimes a writer clearly wants others to read the work. In that case, errors should be minimal. To achieve this higher level of writing, writers edit their work to make corrections, improve the wording, and make the writing ready to be published. This is a final draft.

Editing is a long procedure if done carefully. It does not need to be done for every single piece of writing. When your child has an assignment to be turned in for a grade, that is an important piece of writing which will be read by others. Thus editing becomes a part of the assignment.

Adults must be patient enough to include editing as a vital step in the writing process. To save you and your child tears, make sure you don't schedule writing, editing, and rewriting a long assignment all in the same night.

It helps speed the process if the learner has a formula to follow to add consistency and accuracy. Copy the chart on the right and place it at your child's work space or enlarge it and make a wall poster! Keep this strategy handy for every writing activity until it becomes a habit for your child to use with any final draft.

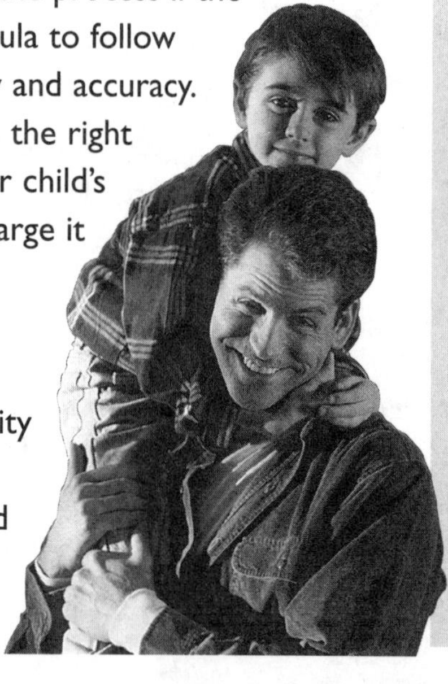

SCOPE IT!
S: Check your sentences.
C: Check the capital letters.
O: Check the order.
P: Check the punctuation.
E: EXCELLENT EDITING!

S is for sentence structure.
* Is every sentence complete?
* Do the sentences make sense?
* Is there a main idea sentence?
* Does each sentence add new information?

C is for capital letters.
* Does every sentence start with a capital letter?
* Do proper nouns (the names of special people, places or things) begin with a capital letter?

O is for order and organization.
* Is there a beginning, middle, and end to the writing?
* Does the order make sense?

P is for punctuation.
* Does every sentence end with the proper punctuation: period, question mark, or exclamation point?
* Are there quotation marks around the exact words someone says?
* Are commas and apostrophes used correctly?

E is for EXCELLENT!

Great job of editing your work! Celebrate and share your work with EVERYONE!!!

SPEAKING UP!

Many times children are expected to share their writing or other work aloud. Speaking to a group or the entire class is an important, and often scary, facet of the language arts curriculum. If your child is afraid to speak up in class, it helps to talk about it. During the conversation, discuss what is the cause of the fear.

If your child is extremely shy, suggest picturing a classroom event in which your child gives a successful report or speaks up successfully in class. Visualization is a technique used by many star athletes that helps them reach their goals.

If other children have laughed at your child, suggest that these students may think laughing at others helps make the teasers braver. Encourage your child to react with humor instead of becoming shy or angry.

If your child thinks he or she is not smart enough to speak up, make a list of all the areas where your child has truly excelled. Express pride in these accomplishments.

If your child is afraid of making a mistake, try these ideas:

* Request that the teacher repeat the question.

* Be sure to be well prepared. Ask yourself questions that the teacher might ask the next day about the material you read.

If your child hates being stared at, teach "deflection" strategies:

* Choose one friend to speak to as you give a report.

* Pick out one face in the back to address.

* Look at the back wall of the room or scan the room with your eyes without really focusing on any one person.

If your child thinks no one is interested in what he or she might say, model interest at home and show that you care about what is said. For example, during a conversation with your child, make sure you are truly focused on your child, not the television or the newspaper.

If your child is still concerned, organize a practice session at home during which you and your child act out

speaking situations. Tell your child that fear can be conquered in this case by even "pretending" that speaking is comfortable. Have your child name a celebrity he or she admires and pretend to be that person giving the talk. Your child can become confident and successful at speaking up even if it is "acting."

What if your child talks too much?

* Model good conversation techniques.

* Point out that good conversation requires taking turns.

* Remind your child to respond to what is said.

* Suggest that your child include questions for the listener.

* Describe conversation as a partnership among two or more people.

* Let your child witness and participate in effective adult conversation.

SILENT ACTION! A VERB GAME

A verb is an action word.

Make grammar practice fun with this game.

1. Write each of these verbs on a separate slip of paper:

   jump   run   drink

   snore   cough   yell

2. Put the slips in a box or basket. Let one member of the family choose a slip.

3. Everyone asks, "What verb did you choose?"

4. The person acts out the verb without a sound! The first person to guess the verb gets the next turn.

Begin with simple verbs and then add more difficult ones. Use words from your child's reading or spelling lists. If your child has difficulty with this game, let him or her select the word from a list of all the verbs in the basket.

> **Verb List Starters:**
>
> Level A: hop, sing, listen, yawn, write
>
> Level B: whisper, scold, think, cut
>
> Level C: trade, accept, brag, choose
>
> Level D: disagree, force, correct, pause

NAME THAT NOUN PROPERLY!

With your child find a place on a map or globe that begins with the same letter as your first name and write a sentence like this: _Sam lives in San Diego_.

Then do the same thing for friends or other people in your family:

Jenni lives in Juneau.

Peter lives in Paris.

Angel lives in Albany.

Chanel lives in Chicago.

Start with a map of just your area, then progress to maps that cover larger and larger areas until you and your child are using a world map. To add variety, use last names to generate the location.

This is a great game to do on a computer or word processor since much of each sentence is repeated. You can just copy and paste and change the name and location. Your child will learn a computer skill and practice proper nouns at the same time. Be sure to show your child how to type capital letters using the keyboard. If you have a CD-ROM atlas or similar software, use it to choose the location.

A noun is the name of a person, place, or thing. A proper noun is the name of a certain person, place, or thing and must begin with a capital letter.

SPELLING

Develop a step-by-step procedure for learning to spell a word. Help your child follow that pattern consistently. Here is a suggested routine. Copy this and place it on the refrigerator right next to the spelling list your child brings home from school.

I can learn to spell any word!

1. I look at the word.
2. I say the word.
3. I write the word.
4. I check the word.
5. I spell the word aloud.
6. I use the word in a sentence.
7. I watch for the word in a book or newspaper.
8. I use the word in a story I am writing.

MY OWN DICTIONARY

Help your child start a dictionary of words that are personal spelling demons. Use a notebook or note pad, or staple 13 sheets of paper together. Label each page with a letter of the alphabet.

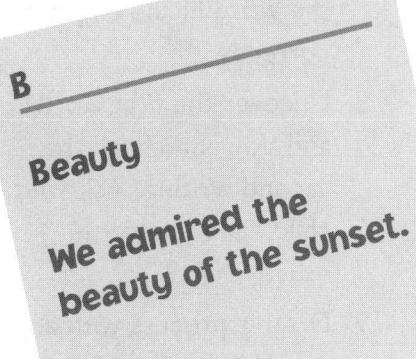

B

Beauty

We admired the beauty of the sunset.

As you review schoolwork, assist with homework, or read a story your child wrote, encourage him or her to jot down any misspelled words.

When any of those words are required again in a piece of writing, the dictionary is there to refer to for the correct spelling. It is quicker than using a large dictionary. Research shows that writers often repeat specific words and this will help your child be assured of accuracy.

Include a short phrase for the meaning of words like *their*, *there*, and *they're*. Homophones

are difficult for third graders to spell correctly.

Be sure your child pronounces words correctly. If you hear "are" when the word should be "our," repeat the sentence and model the correct pronunciation.

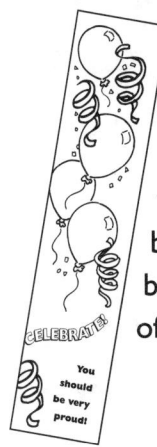

Reward your child's progress in spelling with one of the bookmarks in this book or a special treat of your choice.

SPELLING STRATEGIES

Learning to spell is a journey beginning with the tiniest step toward putting sounds with letters and progressing to formal spelling patterns. Third graders may be at different levels of spelling ability. The ultimate goal for all learners is to spell words correctly.

Help your child practice spelling by using fun activities. Avoid lots of paper and pencil practice which is already utilized at school.

You may want to refer to the page in this book on math facts. Many of the fun ways suggested there to practice facts will work with spelling words as well.

Picture Clues—Many words can be written in a way that will remind the student what the word means and that will give the reader a visual clue to the spelling.

Oral Spelling—Practice words aloud only after your child has seen the word written and has written it independently. Direct your child to spell the whole word. You can spell some of the words, too. Make a mistake once in awhile and see if you get caught! Some children find it helpful to write in the air with their fingers as they spell the word aloud.

Configuration—This is a great visualization technique that creates a picture of the word in the mind of the reader.

1. Use a sheet of half-inch graph paper.
2. Have your child write the word on the graph paper putting one letter in each box. If the letter is tall, give it two boxes. If the letter hangs down, use the box below to complete it.
3. Now show your child how to draw a box around the letters. Tell your child to make square corners.

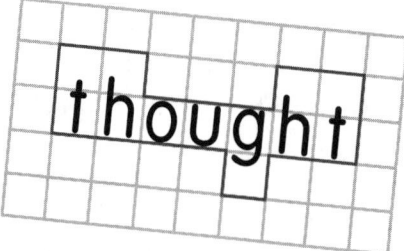

4. Outline the box with a dark marker so it stands out.
5. Now draw another box just like that one somewhere else on the paper.

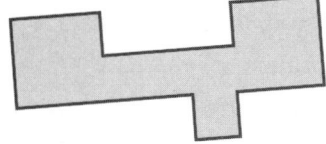

6. Cover up the first word and box.
7. See if your child can write the word in the empty box correctly.
8. Uncover the first word and box and check the second writing. Ask your child, "Did you get it exactly right?"
9. Do this process with any word that is hard for your child to spell.

PENMANSHIP

Learning and practicing cursive handwriting is an important activity in third grade. There are two major styles of cursive handwriting —regular and contempory. Both are included in this book for your reference. Check with your child's teacher to see which style your school uses.

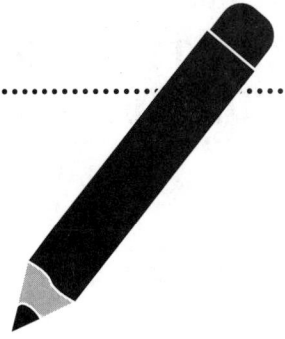

REGULAR CURSIVE

$$Aa \quad Bb \quad Cc \quad Dd$$

$$Ee \quad Ff \quad Gg \quad Hh$$

$$Ii \quad Jj \quad Kk \quad Ll$$

$$Mm \quad Nn \quad Oo \quad Pp$$

$$Qq \quad Rr \quad Ss \quad Tt$$

$$Uu \quad Vv \quad Ww \quad Xx$$

$$Yy \quad Zz$$

CONTEMPORARY CURSIVE

Aa Bb Cc

Dd Ee Ff Gg

Hh Ii Jj Kk

Ll Mm Nn Oo

Pp Qq Rr Ss

Tt Uu Vv Ww

Xx Yy Zz

Math Skills
Third Graders Need

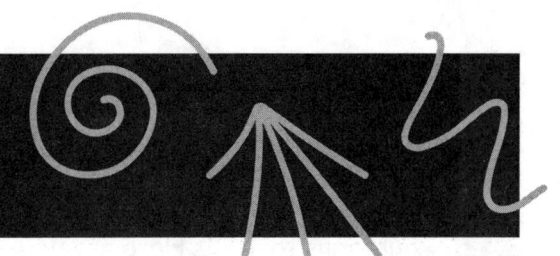

NUMBERS, FACTS, AND COMPUTATION

* Understand place value to one million

* Read and write numbers and number words to one thousand

* Recognize number patterns like these: 2, 3, 5, 6, 8, 9 . . . or 6, 12, 18, 24, 30 . . .

* Round two-digit numbers to the nearest ten

* Master addition facts (0 + 0 through 9 + 9)

* Master subtraction facts (0 – 0 through 18 – 9)

* Practice multiplication facts

* Practice division facts

* Add and subtract 4-digit numbers

* Add three 2-digit numbers

* Rename or regroup (carrying and borrowing)

* Estimate results and check with a calculator

GEOMETRY, MEASUREMENT, AND FRACTIONS

* Understand symmetry where both halves of a shape or object are the same

* Explore shapes with many sides

* Identify and create geometric patterns

* Estimate distances and amounts

* Compare volume

* Measure length, width, and height to the nearest inch or centimeter

* Use metric and customary measuring instruments

* Recognize fractions: ½, ⅓, ¼, ⅛

MONEY, TIME, AND PROBLEM SOLVING

* Name all coins and bills

* Add and subtract dollars and cents

* Make change and practice counting it back

* Tell time to the nearest minute on both analog and digital clocks

* Understand and use a calendar

* Use different strategies for solving problems—guess and check, find a pattern, draw a picture, act it out, write a math sentence

* Be aware of key words that may indicate which operation to use

* Choose the correct operation needed to solve the problem

NUMERATION

Third graders should be able to read and write numerals to 1000. Here are some fun ways to reinforce numeration.

* As you shop at the grocery store, have your child locate items that come in lots of 50, 100, 500, or 1000. Examples: 100 vitamins, 500 cotton swabs. Be sure to note how the amount is written on different products.

* Write an amount of money on a slip of paper, such as $142. Let your child browse through catalogs or newspaper inserts and find something to buy that costs exactly that amount of money or a little less. Vary the amount each time you play.

* Explore a calendar with your child, pointing out the different number of days in each month. Tell your child to estimate how many days there are in a year. Then add up all the days. Check the answer. Be sure your child says "three hundred sixty-five," not "three hundred *and* sixty-five." (The *and* indicates a decimal point.)

* Use play money from a board game you have, such as Monopoly.™ Take turns writing out "bills" to each other listing how much to pay for a chore or activity that was completed that day. Perhaps you owe your child $479 for cleaning the bathrooms and he owes you $392 for making dinner. Each person who receives the bill counts out the amount in play money and has the other person check it. Set the game range between $100 and $1000 to give your child maximum practice.

* Use candies or cereal of different colors to practice making numbers. Jelly beans work great for this. First make a workmat like the one below.

Lay down 1 black, 4 reds, and 2 yellows. Your child should write 142 and read *one hundred forty-two.* Take turns giving each other jelly beans and writing and reading the matching numbers. You may want to have your child gather a handful of jelly beans, sort them, and make the matching number. Whenever there are 10 of one color, your child should trade them (regrouping) for one of the next larger color. Use only one green jelly bean to begin with. Once your child is ready, you can add more greens to make greater numbers.

Jelly Bean Numbers

GREEN thousands	BLACK hundreds	RED tens	YELLOW ones

MEASUREMENT

To demonstrate the importance of using a standard unit when measuring, have your child walk across the room, heel to toe, counting the steps. Now you do the same. Compare answers. Ask your child, "Why are our numbers different?" A similar activity is to use toothpicks laid end to end to measure the length of a piece of paper. Next lay pencils end to end and measure it. Then use a ruler. Why are all the numbers different? Talk about how measuring things this way would not work. If you ordered a board ten feet long measured by your feet, would the carpenter's feet be the same length as yours?

Show your child a yardstick and a meter stick. (Or substitute a ruler or measuring tape that has both Customary and Metric units.) Compare the different markings. Explain that they are two systems of measurement and it is important to be familiar with both. Inches and feet are known as Customary units and centimeters and meters are Metric units. Compare product labels to find other examples of measurement units (Customary—quarts, pounds, ounces; Metric—liters, kilograms, grams).

Measurement Scavenger Hunt—Do this scavenger hunt to practice measurement.

* Find 5 things that are less than a centimeter long.
* Find 5 things that are more than an inch long.
* Find 5 things that are more than a foot long.
* Find 5 things that are less than a meter long.
* Find something that is about 11 inches high.
* Find something that is about 3 centimeters high.
* Find something that is about 6 centimeters around! Do you need a different measuring tool?

Estimate It!—Estimation is an excellent skill to incorporate with measuring activities. Before your child begins measuring items, ask him or her to "guess" or "predict" the length, height, or the width of a particular item. Then suggest measuring to see how close the estimate was to the real measurement.

Which is more?—Save a liter bottle and a quart jar or measuring cup. (Some measuring cups have both measuring systems on them so you can compare them in one step.) Let your child fill the liter bottle with water and then pour it into the quart jar. Are they the same? Would you rather have one liter of soda or one quart of soda or does it make any difference? Pour the water on a thirsty plant or cook some spaghetti in it when you are finished . . . don't waste it!

Make Measuring Memos—Help your child measure one centimeter on a cardboard strip and cut it out. Use that standard to test measure items he or she finds. Do the same for an inch, foot, yard, and meter. To measure an entire room, your child could cut several yard lengths or meter lengths of cardboard or string and lay them end to end. Discuss why having a ruler or measuring tape is handier than a single individual segment.

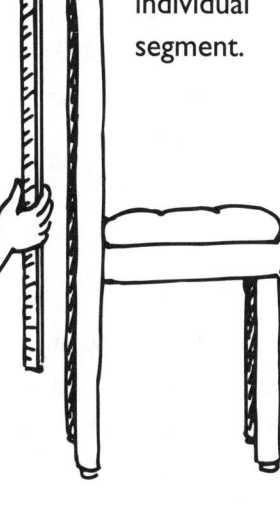

FACTS CAN BE FUN!

Practicing math facts is a very important part of learning. It does not have to be boring if you spice up the practice time with some action! Here are some fun ways to practice math facts.

Beach Ball Toss—Purchase an inflatable plastic beach ball. (At the end of the summer you can find them at bargain prices on the clearance tables of discount stores.) Use a marker to write a fact your child needs to practice on each colored section. Check in your child's math text for samples.

Toss the ball to your child and call out a color. Your child calls out the answer to the fact, tosses the ball back, and calls out a color for you. Once in awhile when it is your turn, call out the wrong answer and see if your child "catches" you in a "miss!"

For variety, put the answer on the ball and have the "catcher" give the problem!

If you use a water-based marker, you can wipe the facts off as they are mastered and add new ones. Water-based markers, however, will rub off on your hands. You may want to purchase several balls and use a permanent marker.

Hopscotch—Draw a hopscotch board on the sidewalk. Write a math fact in each box. Each player tosses a marker and hops down to the box it lands in, saying the answers to the facts as they hop along.

Caution: Have children check their shoes for chalk dust before they enter the house.

Write and Eat—Write the answer to a math fact on a graham cracker with squeeze-tube icing. Have your child give you the problem and then eat the snack! Be sure your child knows what operation (addition, subtraction, multiplication or division) that is being practiced. For a more nutritional approach, use squirtable cheese on crackers.

Stick Writing—While sitting on the beach, in your yard, or in your driveway, write facts and answers in the sand or dirt with a stick.

Kitchen Writing—Fill a cookie sheet with a thin layer of cornmeal, flour, or salt. Instead of writing math facts on paper, have your child write them in the tray with a finger.

Caution: Salt can corrode metal, so don't leave it on the cookie sheet for long periods of time. Don't reuse any of these substances in cooking after using them this way.

MORE MATH FACT FUN!

Eggsactly Correct!—Save an egg carton to use for this activity. (The pastel styrofoam ones work great!) Write a number in each egg cup from 0 to 11. Place two buttons or small rocks inside the egg carton. Shut the lid and hold it tightly while you give it a good shake. Then open it and see where the two rocks have landed. Have your child add, subtract, or multiply the two numbers. If the numbers 0 to 11 create problems too difficult for your child, just repeat the digits the teacher is focusing on in math class.

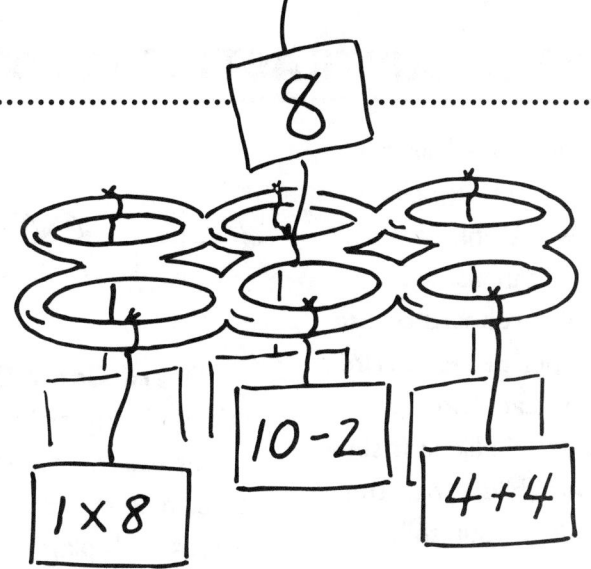

Math Mobile!—Remove the plastic rings from a six pack of your favorite soda. Attach a string or length of fish line to the center. Choose a number for the top of this mobile, such as 8. Have your child write an "8" on a 3" x 2" piece of paper or cardboard. Tape this to the top string. From the edge of each circle, tie another length of string.

Each string should be a different length. On separate pieces of paper, have your child write six math problems that have 8 as the answer. (Examples: 7 + 1, 13 − 5, 2 x 4) Tie or tape each paper to the end of a string. Make several and use them to decorate the ceiling of the playroom or bedroom so your child can practice anytime.

FRIENDLY FAMILY COMPUTATIONS

Help your child write down the ages of everyone in your family. Then make up math questions that relate, such as:

* How much older is your brother than your sister?

* Add the ages of all your aunts and uncles. Is it more than 100? Is it more than 200?

* How many relatives are 10 years older than you are?

* If Uncle George is 42 years old, when was he born?

* Who is the oldest person in the family? How many years older than you is that person?

* What is the average age of everyone in the family? (Add up all the ages and divide by the number of people.)

Try this activity using the ages of friends or neighbors. Your child can interview friends and neighbors to collect data. Neighbors might be interested to know the average age in your neighborhood, the oldest, the youngest, how many neighbors are under 12, and so on. If so, expand this project to include a simple newsletter for all the neighbors. Your child might want to include original drawings or graphs to help people understand the information.

ADDING IT, SUBTRACTING IT, AND MULTIPLYING IT, TOO!

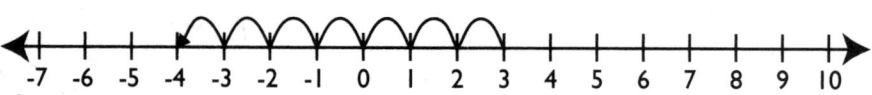

Flying Facts—This is a fun outside game. Use clean pizza circles available at pizza parlors. (You can also cut circles from cardboard or use very stiff paper plates.) Write a math fact on each circle and then toss a circle like a frisbee toward your child. When the circle is caught, your child responds with the answer to the math fact and tosses a circle for you to answer. Each player should have an assortment of 3–5 circles with facts on them.

Board Game Bonanza—While playing ordinary board games use math flash cards to determine the number of spaces each player gets to move.

A pair of dice will work well, too, for game boards. The players must add, subtract, or multiply the numbers represented to decide how far they will move on that turn. This is especially fun if you have die of two colors and set the rule that the "red" number is always first. You may have to move backwards sometimes, since a "red" 3 minus a "green" 7 would give you a ‾4. This may be a bit advanced for third grade, but if you use a number line, it simply becomes a matter of counting backwards. This helps teach your child the concept of negative numbers.

To use the number line: Put your finger on 3 and count backwards 7 spaces. You are below zero on ‾4. So you must back up on the game board 4 spaces.

Calendar Calculations—Write a math problem for your child on each day of the calendar. Sometime during that day, have your child solve it. Draw a star or happy face in the box to indicate success. If nothing appears by the next day, your child will know the answer is incorrect and should try it again (as well as the problem for the current day). At the end of the week or month, reward your child with a trip to the park, a special treat, or by reading an extra chapter to him or her that evening at bedtime. Write brain teaser problems for special events or holidays. Each child in your family could have a different calendar to complete. You can find the problems in your child's math book or consult the teacher for suggestions that would be appropriate.

MONEY MASTERY!

Cafeteria Time—For lunch one day, set up the food on the kitchen counter with price tags, just like you would see in a cafeteria. Give your child some money, pretend or real, and allow your child to figure out how to get the most food for the money! Reverse the roles and let your child be the cashier. Pay extra so that your child will have to make change!

Waiting in the Grocery Line—Be sure to give your child real-life practice with money situations. Have your child go through the checkout lanes to pay for a small amount of groceries. As you wait in line, have your child estimate how much they will cost, determine how much money he or she has, and figure out how much change to expect. Compliment your child when the transaction is completed.

Budgeting—Help your child set up a simple budget for allowance or birthday money. You may want to use the sheet on page 84, *A Beginning Budget*. Have your child fill in the money currently available, projected income, and proposed spending. Let your child design spending categories such as savings, charity, special events, toys, and so on. At the end of the month, have your child write notes comparing the actual income and spending to the proposed. If you keep a budget for your family, show your child how you do it. After operating on a budget for awhile, have your child evaluate how it worked. Ask questions such as:

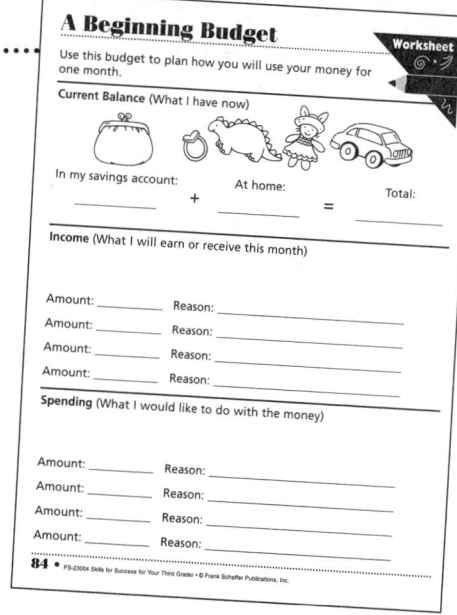

* Did having a budget help you plan how to use your money?

* Would you want to make any changes to your budget?

* For whom else might your budget work? Who would need a different budget?

PROBABILITY

Heads and Tails—Play a quick game of heads and tails by tossing a coin in the air and letting your child call "heads" or "tails" before it lands. Do this 10 times. Using a tally sheet or bar graph, mark the results of each toss. Have your child review the graph and decide which happens more frequently. Then try it 10 more times. Discuss why it turned out the same or different. Ask your child if it would matter if someone else tossed the coin. Analyzing information is an important skill for students to practice in real-life situations.

Heads	✔			✔		✔		✔	✔	
Tails		✔	✔		✔		✔			✔

STORY PROBLEMS

Teachers will tell you that the most difficult math activity for most students is solving story problems. One reason is that many children do not think through which operations make sense in solving the problem—addition, subtraction, multiplication, or division. A basic concept children should know is that adding or multiplying whole numbers yields equal or greater numbers. Subtracting or dividing yields equal or lesser numbers.

The more practice children have with story problems, the easier they become. When practicing story problems with your child, there are two things to keep in mind:

1. You need to teach strategies to help your child think through and solve the problems.

2. You need to use real-life situations. Use topics that interest your child and personalize them. If you are solving a problem that your child could solve, invite him or her to help you.

Examples:

Problem-solving Strategies
- Recognize clue words
  Addition—altogether; in all, total
  Subtraction—left, how many more, difference
  Multiplication—altogether; How many in all the sets?
  Division—How many in each set or group?
- Choose an operation $(+ - \times \div)$
- Find a pattern
- Draw a picture
- Act it out with objects
- Guess and check

1. (Your child's name) has in-line skates with 8 wheels on each one. How many wheels are there altogether on the skates? *16 wheels* (8 + 8 = 16 or 8 x 2 = 16; Point out that a problem can often be solved in more than one way.)

2. (Your child's name) has 23 pieces of candy. (A friend of your child) has 17 pieces of candy. How much more candy does (your child) have than (your child's friend)? *6 pieces more* (23 − 17 = 6)

3. Every child in the first row in the third grade classroom at (your child's school) has 4 yellow pencils. There are 6 children in the first row. If they put all their pencils together in one pencil box, how many pencils would there be? *24 pencils* (4 + 4 + 4 + 4 + 4 + 4 = 24 or 4 x 6 = 24)

4. At lunch, (your child's name) wants to share his/her bag of marshmallows with (friend) and (friend). There are 18 marshmallows in the bag. How many will each child get? *6 marshmallows* (18 ÷ 3 = 6)

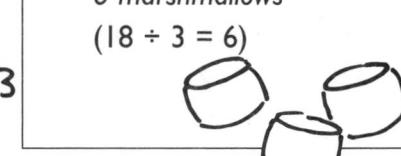

Remember, pictures often get the message across better than words. Have your child draw a picture of what the problem is describing and what it is asking. It can be just a quick sketch that will add meaning to help determine which operation to use.

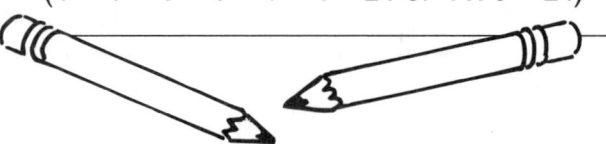

Science and Health Skills Third Graders Need

LIFE SCIENCE, EARTH SCIENCE, AND PHYSICAL SCIENCE

* Predict
* Observe
* Classify and measure
* Collect and organize data
* Draw conclusions
* Understand seeds and the process of germination
* Understand the difference between living and non-living
* Understand the food chain
* Understand the difference between plants and animals

* Understand the water cycle
* Identify different types of rocks
* Identify phases of the moon
* Identify planets in the solar system
* Define the three major states of matter

* Classify changes as physical or chemical
* Understand a force is something that causes a change in motion or shape
* Recognize that magnetism and gravity are forces

HEALTH AND SAFETY

* Recognize the importance of fitness
* Identify healthy foods needed for a balanced diet

* Identify the function of these body systems: skeletal, respiratory, muscular, and circulatory
* Identify good dental health actions
* Understand how to control germs
* Identify careers in the health profession
* Be aware of harmful health practices, including drug and alcohol abuse
* Understand and respect the power of electricity
* Know safety rules regarding

* bike and pedestrian travel
* Know emergency procedures, such as calling 911
* Know and practice firesafety procedures
* Follow safety rules when playing
* Know how to handle being approached by a stranger
* Know what to do if someone touches them in an inappropriate way
* Know home safety rules, such as letting parents/guardians know where they are at all times

LIVING AND NON-LIVING

Learning about the world around them is an important part of what third graders study in science classes. You can help your child by providing home experiences to support the school objectives.

Take a walk with your child around the house and outdoors. Locate an example of each of the characteristics below to demonstrate the difference between living and non-living.

Characteristic
* Living things grow, change, and repair themselves

Activities
* find a puppy and a dog
* look at a tiny plant and a large one
* find a tree where a branch broke off
* place a dry lima bean inside a plastic bag with a damp paper towel and watch it germinate

Characteristic
* Living things are made of cells

Activities
* scrape the inside of your cheek with a clean swab, rub the swab on a slide, and look at it under a microscope or very strong magnifying glass
* look at pictures of cells in an encyclopedia or science textbook

Characteristic
* Living things need energy

Activities
* discuss why we eat food
* talk about how plants get energy from the sun

Characteristic
* Living things respond to their environment

Activity
* set a plant in front of a bright window, watch it bend and grow toward the sunlight over a period of time

Characteristic
* Living things reproduce and create new life

Activities
* observe new plant sprouts
* look for baby animals in books, your neighborhood, or at the zoo
* talk about humans and their babies

Picture Fun—Encourage your child to find pictures or draw pictures of living and non-living things. Mark "L" on the living items in the picture and "N" on the non-living items.

A Terrific Terrarium—Create a terrarium in a large glass jar or aquarium. Put a layer of gravel in the bottom, next a layer of sand, and then a layer of potting soil. Add one or two small plants and some rocks. Talk about the difference between living and non-living. Introduce an earthworm or two and observe. Keep the terrarium covered unless condensation appears, then uncover it for a short time.

Brain Teaser: Gather a few non-living objects such as a pencil, a rock, and a hammer. Ask your child, "Were any parts of these items ever living?" (Remind your child that wood comes from trees!)

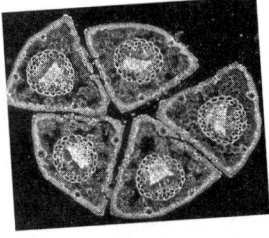

ROCKS AND SOIL

The best way to help your child learn about rocks and soil is to visit a variety of locations and dig around.

* At the park or near a lake, find a safe, little-traveled roadway or driveway filled with rocks. Work together to collect a variety of rocks and then classify them by color, size, shape, texture, or type.

* Read *Everybody Needs a Rock* by Byrd Baylor (Scribner, 1974). Discuss it with your child to increase awareness of the importance of our land and soil as a natural resource.

* Give your child two rocks that seem porous or crumbly. Holding the rocks above a dark piece of paper, let your child rub the two rocks together. By using a magnifying glass, your child will soon see that the sand on the paper is actually tiny rocks. This project demonstrates that soil is actually made of rocks being weathered and worn. Wind, water, and friction (such as your child has just created), cause that erosion of rock into soil. Point out that some rocks are very soft, like chalk, and wear down quickly. Others are very hard, like granite or marble, and erode very slowly over thousands of years.

* Visit an agricultural office or nursery. They may have soil samples you can observe. Notice the color and texture differences.

* Place about 1 cup of soil in a quart jar of water. Put the lid on tight and shake it hard. Let it sit overnight without being moved. Notice the layers that have settled. The bottom layer will be sand and gravel, the middle layers will be silt and clay, and the top layer will be loam and humus. This lets your child see the types of soil you have in your area.

* Soil takes thousands of years to form so humans must use the land wisely. Watch for examples of ways people are using the land carefully such as terracing the land or planting windbreaks. Let your child fill a shallow plastic box or tray with sand or soil and add plastic trees, houses, and figures from the toy box. Stand back about 3 feet and aim a hair dryer at the box. Your child will quickly see the loss of soil that comes from wind. Tilt the box and repeat the experiment using a garden hose first with little water pressure and then with more pressure. Let your child try to replace the figures in a different way to prevent soil erosion.

SOLAR SYSTEM

With the excitement of continued space exploration filling the headlines, it is no wonder third graders are thrilled when the teacher announces they will be studying the planets. Prepare your child for this unit by spending some delightful evenings outside gazing at the stars. If you live in a large city, you may need to drive to a rural area to see well.

✳ Together read *The Magic School Bus Lost in the Solar System* by Joanna Cole (Scholastic, 1990). Enjoy the adventures within the pages and encourage questions about facts or information your child may not understand.

✳ Explain to your child that the sun is a huge star that is actually 93 million miles away. Our planet revolves around the sun. Because Earth is tilted on its axis as it revolves around the sun, different parts get more or less sunshine during different times of the year. That is what causes seasons. When our part of Earth is tilted towards the sun, it is summer. When it is tilted away from the sun, it is winter. You can demonstrate this by setting a flashlight or lamp in the center of the room. Have your child label a ball with the equator, your location, and the North Pole. Direct your child to tilt the ball slightly, hold it at chest level, and walk around the light. Be sure the path is slightly elliptical, or oval-shaped, and not a circle. Compare the different amounts of sunshine the ball gets as it travels.

✳ At the same time that Earth is revolving, it is also rotating, or spinning around on its axis. This creates day and night. Your child can turn slowly as he or she walks around the lamp to visualize this process.

CONSTELLATIONS

As you gaze at the stars, tell your child to connect the dots in the sky and make pictures. Help them pick out well known constellations such as the Big Dipper and Little Dipper. You may need to draw a picture of a dipper on paper before your child will be able to spy it up in the sky!

✳ At home, cut a black circle ¾" larger than the end of a cardboard tube. Use a push pin to punch out a real or invented constellation in the middle of the black circle. Use as few holes as possible and keep the design simple. Then wrap the black circle over the end of the tube and fasten it with a rubber band. Point it toward a strong light and see your constellation come to life.

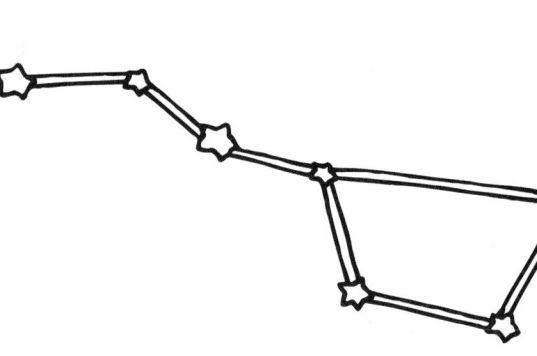

MATTER REALLY MATTERS!

In many schools, third graders begin to explore the states of matter: liquids, solids, and gases. The more experiences you can provide to help your child discover the properties of these three states, the more quickly your child will connect with information provided in the classroom.

Characteristics of a solid:

✳ comes in different shapes and doesn't change shape easily

✳ can usually be seen

✳ is constructed of particles called molecules that are packed tightly together and do not move or move very slowly

Examples: ice, bricks, your hand

Characteristics of a liquid:

✳ can be poured and changes shape easily

✳ can usually be seen

✳ is constructed of particles called molecules that move and are not packed so tightly together as in a solid

Examples: milk, water, oil

Characteristics of a gas:

✳ can not always be seen but takes up space

✳ changes shape very easily

✳ is constructed of particles called molecules that are far apart and moving very quickly

Examples: air, helium, water vapor

The simplest way to demonstrate all three is to place an ice cube in a dish. While it is frozen, it is a solid. When it melts, it is a liquid. When it evaporates, it is a gas. Ask your child, "What causes the solid to become a liquid? What causes the liquid to become a gas?" Be sure to point out that heat created both changes.

WHAT MATTER IS IT?

Help your child identify the different states of matter. Select three containers you cannot see through. (Film canisters or yogurt cups with lids work well.) While your child is not watching, place rocks in one container, fill another ⅔ full of water, and leave the third "empty."

Using three small cards, have your child write *Solid* on one, *Liquid* on another, and *Gas* on the third. Allow your child to shake, listen, and examine the containers without removing the lids. After making a decision, have your child place the container on the card that names the matter inside. Ask your child to explain his or her reasoning. Refer to the descriptions on this page as a review if necessary. Now open the lids and congratulate your child's ability to discover information.

Make it harder! While your child is not watching, replace the rocks with cotton balls. Leave the other containers the same but move them around.

(This is why it is important that all three containers are exactly alike.) Now let your child try to determine the three states of matter. Discuss your child's reasoning. Then let your child find examples and test you!

MYSTERY MATTER—IS IT SOLID OR LIQUID?

Pour a half box of cornstarch into a plastic bowl. Begin stirring in water very slowly and mixing well until the mixture is wet but not runny. It usually takes less than a cup, but can vary in different locations. It should flow when you pick it up, but it also should break off. It acts like a solid and a liquid. Ask your child: Do you think it is a liquid or a solid? Why? How would it feel to wade in this?

You can add tempera paint or food coloring as you add the water to the cornstarch to create a mystery color, too. Clean up is easy; it brushes off just like dry cornstarch. Cover it tightly when not in use. It will dry some overnight, but add a drop of water to revive it and you'll all have many more hours of fun.

CHANGES IN MATTER

Matter can change in two ways.

1. **Physical Change**—When matter undergoes a physical change, it changes form but it remains the item it was before. Some examples of physical changes are water freezing, a board being cut, or a piece of paper being torn.

2. **Chemical Change**—When matter undergoes a chemical change, it takes on different characteristics than the original matter. When unprotected metal is left to weather, it rusts. Rust is a different matter than the metal was. When paper is burned, it becomes ash. Ash is a different matter than the paper was.

Change Some Matter—Let your child create physical changes in matter by working with clay or play dough. Have your child change the shape and size of the matter to make different objects. Then demonstrate both physical and chemical changes to your child by tearing and burning paper.

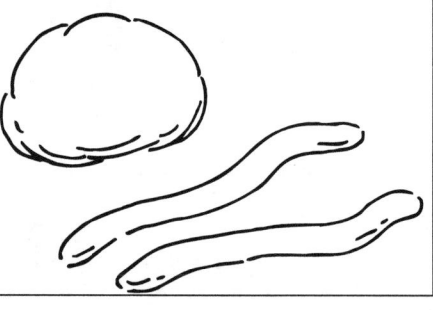

Watch the Balloon—Do this experiment together to show another form of chemical change.

Materials needed: empty plastic soda bottle, baking soda, vinegar, balloon

1. Put a teaspoon of baking soda in the empty bottle.
2. Add a teaspoon of vinegar.
3. Quickly place a balloon over the lip of the bottle.
4. Watch what happens.

Results: The balloon expands because the two substances had a chemical reaction and created a gas.

If you have a large balloon and a large bottle, use a greater amount of each substance to allow the balloon to expand even more.

MAGNETS

One force at work in our world is magnetism. People use magnets in many items, such as tools, appliances, machinery, and even videotapes. Help your child experiment with magnets in these activities. You'll want to collect several magnets, preferably in different styles, such as bar magnets and horseshoe magnets, to enhance the projects. However, if you only have access to one magnet, most of the ideas will still work.

✳ Place a pin or staple on a table and cover it with a plain piece of paper. Let your child pick up the pin with a magnet. The paper will lift, too.

✳ See how many pins or small nails your magnet will lift. Try different magnets of different strengths and styles. Which one lifts the most?

✳ Ask your child to collect a variety of household items that might be attracted to a magnet. Then test each object and see if the predictions hold true. Next have your child select objects that might not be attracted to a magnet. Test the predictions. You can use page 88 to record results.

✳ Glue a paper clip on the back of a cut out fish. Hold a piece of blue paper behind the fish. Behind the paper hold a magnet. You can make the fish "swim" in the "water" by using the magnet's attraction to the paper clip.

GRAVITY

Gravity is the force that pulls us toward the center of the earth. Without it, objects would float around as they sometimes do in space. Let your child experience the force of gravity with these activities and discover the science around them.

✳ Select several items of different weight, such as a rock, sponge, feather, block of wood, tissue, and book. Take turns standing on a chair and dropping the items in pairs. Gravity pulls all the objects to the earth. Ask your child how an object's shape affects whether it falls slower or faster than another object.

✳ For a humorous look at life without gravity, read aloud the book *The Light Princess* retold by Robin McKinley (Harcourt Brace Jovanovich, 1988).

✳ Place a mound of clay or wet sand on a tray on the floor. Smooth the surface. Have your child hold a large marble at waist-height and drop it onto the tray. Then have your child drop it from shoulder-height. Examine and compare the two craters. Next have your child stand on a chair to drop the marble. Again examine and compare the craters. Ask your child questions such as: Which crater was the deepest? Why do you think that crater was deeper than the others? Did the width of the craters change? Repeat the activity using different sized balls—large, small, heavy, light. Have your child make some predictions and then test them.

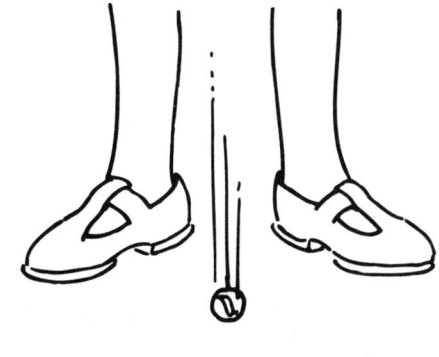

FABULOUS FOOD ACTIVITIES

Third Graders are able to understand that food gives us energy. They also can learn that in order to be healthy we all need to make wise choices about the kinds and amounts of food we eat.

Grocery Trip—The best way to help your child learn about food choices is on your regular trip to the grocery store.

✳ If you would like to get nutrition education information before you go, here are some resources to contact:

- your county or state department of Consumer and Family Education

- your local or national 4-H program

- the National Dairy Council 800-426-8271

These resources have pamphlets, charts, and recipes. Some are available for a small fee. Be sure to mention the grade level of your child so the materials will be appropriate.

✳ Teach your child how to read the nutrition labels found on food products. Point out how ingredients are listed in order from greatest amount to least.

Select two or three boxes of cereal and ask your child to determine which has less sugar in it.

✳ If your child gets to select a snack product on this grocery trip, require the selection of at least one healthy snack or direct the selection to come from a specific food group. For example, your child could choose a fruit or select a dairy product like yogurt or pudding.

FUN AT HOME

✳ Eating a variety of food is another important health consideration. Let your child taste test foods by frequently including a new item in the evening meal. Limit the new additions to no more than one per meal.

✳ Children are more inclined to taste new foods if they are involved in the

preparation. Let your child help clean the fresh vegetables and begin to learn the steps involved in cooking some dishes. (ADULT SUPERVISION IS NECESSARY FOR THIS.)

✳ Make new foods fun. Let your child try adding a drop of food coloring to the cream cheese on the bagel or bread. Cut eyes and a

mouth out of a cheese slice, lay it on a bun, and warm it slightly.

✳ Though many of us grew up learning the four food groups, children today use a food pyramid to learn about a balanced diet. Have your child compare the food he or she eats in a day to the recommended amounts.

Social Studies Skills Third Graders Need

GEOGRAPHY, COMMUNITY, AND HERITAGE

* Locate their city, state, and country on a map

* Locate the United States on a globe

* Identify directions (N, S, E, and W) on a map

* Use a compass rose

* Interpret map symbols

* Begin to understand scale

* Create a map of a familiar area

* Identify the continents

* Know that about three-fourths of the earth is covered by water

* Explain geographical terms like river, lake, ocean, coast, island, mountain, forest, desert, and plain

* Understand that warmer climates are found near the equator and cooler climates occur near the poles

* Describe a community

* Describe the need for shelter, food, and clothing for all people

* Identify workers in a community

* Describe differences between rural and urban neighborhoods

* Identify different modes of transportation and the purpose of each

* Be aware of current events that involve their community

* Identify personal cultural heritage

* Express knowledge and interest in a variety of cultural holidays

* Value the diversity and recognize the commonality of ethnic groups and cultures within our country

* Recognize the purpose of national holidays

* Tell the importance of July 4

* Identify the contributions of famous Americans, such as George Washington, Abraham Lincoln, Susan B. Anthony, and Martin Luther King, Jr.

GOVERNMENT, ECOLOGY, AND GRAPHS

* Explain the reason for laws

* Discuss the fact that government leaders in the U.S. are elected

* Name a local leader

* Name the current U.S. president

* Know there are 50 states in the U.S.

* Know their own city, state, and state capital

* Explain the importance of conserving our natural resources

* Explain the meaning of "Reduce, Reuse, and Recycle"

* Interpret bar graphs

* Explain how a graph helps us understand information

* Begin to comprehend a circle graph

MAP SKILLS

Third graders are expected to begin to master some basic map skills that were introduced in earlier grades. Skills like interpreting symbols, understanding a legend, understanding scale, and using directions to locate places are critical to success in the social studies areas. You can help your child by using these skills in familiar and important settings.

Bedroom Map—Start by helping your child construct a flat map of his or her room. You may be planning to lay new carpet or rearrange the furniture. If so, get your child involved in the measuring and transferring of that information to paper.

Explain that this map is made as though you are sitting on the ceiling and looking down at the room. Encourage your child to design symbols that would indicate toy boxes, shelves, windows, doors, bed, chair, desk, or dresser. Using graph paper may make it easier for your child to draw items.

Street Map—Help your child design a simple map to show the way to school. Emphasize these items that help prevent the map user from getting lost: 1) a compass rose to indicate directions, and 2) clearly labeled streets. If possible, use the map and actually follow it. See if you and your child end up at school. Have your child make any necessary corrections and try it again!

Family Map—Have your child draw a rough map of your coummunity, state, or country, labeling where you and some of your favorite relatives live.

Direction Directions—Discuss with your child which way is north, south, east, and west in your house or yard. Play a "Simon Says" game using directions. Remind players to do only what "Simon Says" to do. Sample directives:

Simon says, "Walk 3 steps north."

Simon says, "Skip 4 steps east."

Simon says, "Walk 1 step south."

Simon says, "Walk 2 steps west."

In the beginning, you may need to write the direction words on index cards and actually lay them on the floor or grass in the matching locations. With enough practice, your child will know the correct way to move. If there are landforms or landmarks in your community that will help with directions, make sure to teach them. Examples: The mountains are west of town. The coast is south of here. The capital building is east of our neighborhood.

Hint: Help your child remember the clockwise order of the directions with this saying, "Never Eat Sour Watermelon!" (North, East, South, West)

LANDFORMS

As you travel long distances or just around your area, point out to your child how the land changes. Ask questions, such as these: Did you notice we have to go up a hill to get to school? Did you see how the river that we crossed on the north edge of our city is the same river we cross on the south edge? Do you remember how different the soil was when we visited the ocean?

Children, like all learners, remember information best when they actually get involved with hands-on projects. To teach your child about landforms, first drive around your area and observe the rivers, lakes, mountains, forests, or other landforms found there. If your area does not offer much variation, use an atlas, globe or a CD-Rom atlas to help your child visualize the differences.

Then let your child create a dough map on cardboard to illustrate a variety of landforms. Begin by making a batch of this dough. If you want a large or complex map, double the recipe.

How to Make a Dough Map

1. Cut a piece of heavy cardboard the size you want. About 12" x 18" or larger will work well.

2. Draw a rough sketch of the map you want to create. Your map can be of your community, state, country, or a make-believe place. Label the landforms you plan to include, such as rivers, forests, and mountains.

3. Place the dough on the cardboard. Spread it over the cardboard creating the landforms you labeled.

4. Keep the map on a flat surface and let it dry for at least two days. After it is completely dry, paint the areas with tempera or water colors.

5. Share the map with friends and classmates. Allow them to "feel" the landforms and describe how each one is unique.

Map Dough

1 cup flour

⅓ cup salt

½ cup water

4 drops of vegetable oil

Combine the flour and salt in a large bowl. Slowly add the water and stir. If it is too dry, add a bit more water. If it is too wet, sprinkle with flour. Stir well. Place the dough on waxed paper and knead. You may need to sprinkle the paper with a bit of flour. This dough hardens if left uncovered. Store in a tightly covered bowl or plastic zippered bag. If you want to keep it for several days, store it in the refrigerator.

COMMUNITY

Living and working with others in a community is a lifetime skill your third grader will need to master. It involves appreciating and respecting the feelings, heritage, and careers of other people, as well as expressing pride in the heritage and career of his or her own family. You can help your child learn to live and work in a community by providing experiences with community life.

Ant Farm—Set up an ant farm so that your child can observe the way ants create a community. Select a book from the public library or use the encyclopedia to describe the variety of jobs and chores that various ants assume. Explain how worker ants build the tunnels, nurse ants care for the young, the queen ant lays the eggs, and soldier ants guard the hill. As you discover how ants function in a community, build upon that information to help explain the larger communities that will be a part of your child's future. Have your child compare how ant and human communities are alike and how they are different.

Links in the Chain—A community needs all kinds of workers to meet the needs of its members and prosper. Brainstorm with your child a list of community workers—teachers, musicians, garbage collectors, doctors, park managers, and so on. Cut strips of paper. On each strip, have your child write the title of a community worker and draw pictures to match. Glue the strip ends together to make links and the links together to make a chain.

Which Community?—To illustrate the various levels of community of which your child is a member, make a list starting with family, neighborhood, city, county, state, country, planet, and galaxy. There are many other communities your third grader belongs to, such as his or her class at school, your place of worship, the Scout Group or 4-H Club, or the neighborhood soccer team.

A community is a group of people (or sometimes animals) that live and work together to help all members of the community.

When the list is complete, draw a small circle in the middle of a huge piece of paper. (Newsprint is inexpensive and works great for this project.) In the center of the circle, have your child write his or her name. Then direct your child to draw another circle around that for the names of family members. Repeat the procedure and have your child fill in the next circle with the names of classmates. Continue out as far as your child has room, filling in circles with names of neighbors, local citizens, and so on.

People in Phoenix

Mrs. Bissett's Class

Mom · Dad

Elysse

Katie

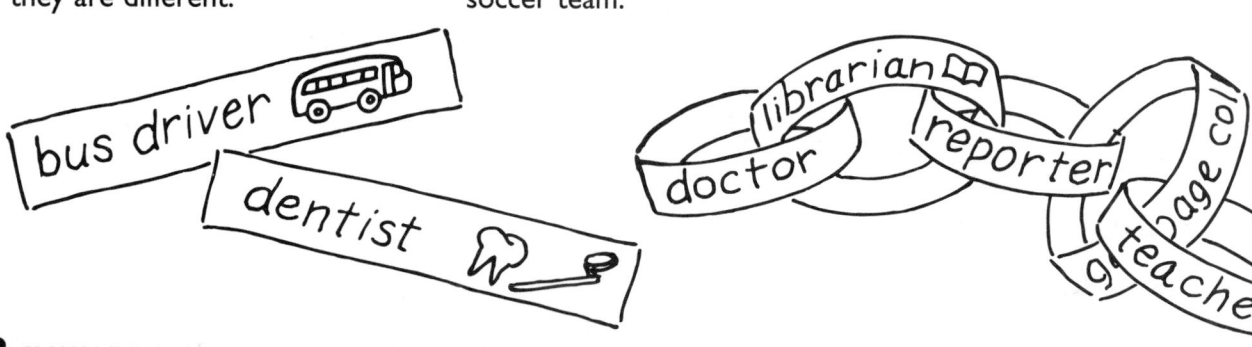

CITIZENSHIP

The goal of good citizenship training is to create involved and knowledgeable leaders and citizenry for our future. You can help your child develop those skills by serving as a role model of an active and respectful citizen.

* Take your child to City Hall or the County Courthouse. Sign up for a tour if one is offered. If possible, have your child meet some of the community's leaders there.

* Create a family compact of rules and laws. Get everyone involved and accept ideas from everyone. Write them on a poster and display them where family members can view them daily. These rules will differ for each family.

occasionally to review the rules and make changes. You can even hold an election to choose the "mayor" or the "secretary" for your family. Parents don't always have to be the leaders.

* Take your child with you when you vote. Discuss the issues and candidates beforehand. Explain your beliefs and encourage your child to share his or her opinions.

* Visit with your child about your volunteer activities in your community. Explain that everyone has the responsibility to participate in order for the community to thrive.

* Find a way that your child can get involved in volunteer activities within your community. Perhaps your child could become involved in a service project through a scout troop, school group, or community club. Charity organizations often need volunteers. Or contact your city hall, local chamber of commerce, or place of worship for ideas.

The members of this family promise to
. . . respect each other's ideas
. . . share time and talents
. . . be responsible for chores
. . . be considerate of each other
. . . be ready on time
. . . help one another

Express the things that are important to you as a family. Make rules for things that have not worked well in the past. Keep the rules short and easy to understand. Meet

Help your child select a service activity that centers around his or her interests. For example, if your child loves animals, perhaps the local Humane Society could use a helper for cleaning and feeding the animals there. If your child likes gardening or planting, the park service in your city or a local senior citizens' home may appreciate help weeding and nurturing the flower plots. Explore the possibilities!

GRAPHS

Many third-grade texts include bar graphs and circle graphs to help students interpret and visualize information. It takes many experiences with these graphs before a student can utilize them easily and benefit from the information that is presented. You can help your child become familiar with graphs by using that as a means of explaining day-to-day information.

✳ Start by pointing out graphs in newspapers and magazines. Pick simple ones that are attempting to make only one point. Your child needs to know that this is an important skill that he or she will use as an adult.

✳ Look for opportunities to create graphs. For example, when your child goes trick or treating at Halloween or when your child buys a bag of candy with a variety of shapes and colors, it is a perfect time to make a bar graph.

✳ Keep a record of the high temperatures each day for a month. Then create a bar graph to show how many days the high temperature was 51–60 degrees, 61–70 degrees, 71–80 degrees, or 81–90 degrees. You could also create a line graph and plot the high temperature each day for a week. These graphs will be easier to make if you use graph paper.

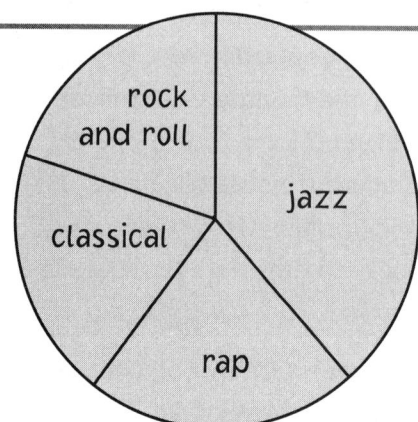

What is your favorite type of music?		
II	jazz	Mom, Paul
I	rock and roll	Dad
I	classical	James
I	rap	Lisa

✳ Introduce circle graphs by making simple ones to represent beliefs or characteristics of your family. First ask a question such as "What is your favorite type of music?" Write the answer of each family member and tally any repeat answers. Next draw a circle and divide it into equal sections corresponding to the number of people in your family. Fill in each section with the matching answer, making sure to group same answers next to each other. Erase repeat labels and dividing lines between sections if the answer is the same. Color different answers on the graph with different colors.

HERITAGE APPRECIATION

To create a sense of roots and belonging, it is important that your child understand and appreciate the heritage that is your family's legacy. You can help your child have a new awareness of this heritage by sharing information about the ancestry and history of your family.

My Tree-mendous Family—This is a fun family project. Outside on the ground, find a small tree limb with several branches. (Or you can purchase one at a craft store.) Anchor the limb in a pot with rocks, soil, or plaster. Cut out a leaf for each member of your family. Write the name of the relative or ancestor on the leaf and designate the relationship to your child(ren). Example: Anna McCrenna—Grandmother.

Punch a hole in the end of each leaf. Insert a twist tie and fasten the leaf to the tree. You may want to have a special family dinner and invite relatives over to see your tree.

Memory Wall—If you have a garage or basement area with a smooth but unfinished wall, invite each relative who comes to visit you to write a memory of their childhood on the wall. Your child can add to the wall with a memory of his or her own at any time. Use a permanent black marker and be sure it is a surface that won't need to be finished later. The marker will show through paint unless you add several coats. If a real wall is not available, put a piece of poster board or paper on a wall and let relatives add their short story on it.

Family Scrapbook—Send a loose-leaf page of a notebook to each living relative and request a story from their childhood. Be sure to ask them to date the occasion. Photos would add a special touch if they could send those. As the stories return, insert them in chronological order in the notebook. On a front page,

create a family tree and put a star beside the name of each person who has contributed. This may become so comprehensive that you will want to consider publishing it for other family members.

Where Did Our Family Come From?—When your child asks that question, make a list of the origins of different family members. Then head for the library or an encyclopedia and help your child locate information about the different groups.

Finding out about costumes, food, dances, games, history, and traditions of your own and other cultures can be an exciting adventure for the whole family. You may discover a custom that you would like to incorporate into your current holiday celebrations.

IT'S IN THE NEWS!

Being informed is a critical part of being a good citizen. The local newspaper can provide you with an important link to your community. But don't limit your thinking to just current events. Lots of ideas for learning are right there in your daily newspaper! This is a great way to model reading for your child. Seeing you reading says that reading is an important, lifetime activity. Here are some other newspaper activities that you and your child can do together:

* Examine the different parts of the newspaper. Share your favorite part with your child.

* Scan headlines to find news stories that interest your child or involve your community.

* Look at photographs and read the captions.

* Show your child the parts of a news article including the headline (the eye-catcher), the byline (author), the dateline (date and location where the story originated), and the lead (the first sentence that is used to grab the reader's attention and convey the most important information). Use a variety of colored markers and let your child mark each part of a story in a different color. Be sure to use an old newspaper that everyone is finished reading!

* Introduce these types of newspaper articles:
a) Hard News Story—Gives facts about important or timely events; b) Feature Story—Gives information about a topic or person of interest to the community; usually written in a friendlier style; and c) Editorial—Gives opinions; may also use facts to try to convince the reader. Then share articles you come across that would be of interest to your child.

* If your child feels strongly about a community topic, encourage him or her to write a letter to the editor. First read sample letters and talk about what makes an effective letter.

* Do a Newspaper Scavenger Hunt! Choose several items from the list below and have your child locate them in the newspaper. It is also fun to get other children involved and make it a team race! Be sure each child has a complete newspaper. If your newspaper focuses on different topics during the week (Monday—science, Tuesday—business, and so on), plan accordingly.

Newspaper Scavenger Hunt

1. Find a picture of a child.
2. Find the predicted high temperature for the day.
3. Find a science word.
4. Find a picture of a food from the bread/grains group.
5. Find the name of your city or state.
6. Find a contraction.
7. Find the name of an athlete or team you like.
8. Find a story about a farm.
9. Find a compound word.
10. Find the name of a school.

Art Skills Third Graders Need

Third graders enjoy art experiences and with their increased fine motor skills, they are ready for more involved processes. They also are excited about the results they produce.

At this age, they are becoming more aware of the world around them and are expanding their horizons to include appreciation of fine arts, diversity of cultural arts, feeling tones that art exhibits, and knowledge of the masters.

* Develop an awareness of art in nature

* Explore two-dimensional processes like drawing, painting, collage, mosaic, printmaking, and rubbings

* Examine the elements of design

* Incorporate different types of line in an original art work

* Understand the concept of space

* Use color hues and shades to create a variety of effects

* Experiment with textures

* Explore three-dimensional processes like clay sculpture and paper sculpture

* Experience weaving and stitchery

* Appreciate the individuality of art creations

* Demonstrate an increased sensitivity to what is art

* Explore emotions created by art

* Become aware of the work of some of the master artists

* Understand the difference between an original piece of art work and a reproduction

ARTISTIC ADVENTURES

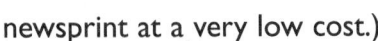

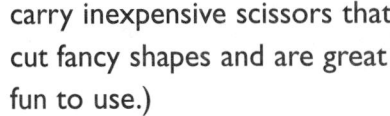

Art expression is a spontaneous adventure that can occur almost anytime. Perhaps your child has just seen a beautiful butterfly and would like to create a similar pattern. Perhaps you and your child have just shared a wonderful story that inspired a picture. Whatever the occasion, be ready! Collect these things and keep them in an Art Box for those special times:

* Drawing paper of all sizes, colors, and types; odds 'n' ends; envelopes—lined and plain (Newspaper publishers often offer roll ends of newsprint at a very low cost.)

* All types of writing instruments—markers, crayons, pencils, chalk

* Clay or homemade dough (Mix I cup flour, ½ cup salt, I tablespoon alum, I tablespoon salad oil, I cup <u>boiling</u> water, and I teaspoon food coloring. Store in airtight container. Do *not* refrigerate.)

* Scissors—plain and fancy (The children's departments of many discount stores now carry inexpensive scissors that cut fancy shapes and are great fun to use.)

* Paint—water colors, tempera, or finger paint

* Paint tools—brushes, cotton swabs, feathers, sponges, string

* Boutique items—old jewelry, sequins, ribbons and trims, boxes, magazines

* Glue—school glue, craft glue, glue sticks (Glitter glue is fun, too!)

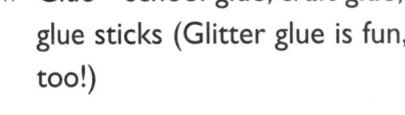

CRAYON CREATIONS

Melted Crayon Design—(BE SURE AN ADULT IS PRESENT AT ALL TIMES!) Light a used candle. Set it on an old cloth or newspaper. Peel the paper off some old crayons. Do *not* use short pieces. Hold the crayon in the flame until it starts to drip and then let the melted wax drip on the paper to make a design. Small projects are better done this way as it is a slow process.

Crayon Resist—Have your child create a simple design or picture on white paper. Direct your child to color over the design with dark, heavy crayon strokes. When the picture is complete, paint over it using a very light tempera or water color. This is a great technique for an ocean creation. Color bright tropical fish and wash over it with a light blue paint. Place plastic wrap over the front, frame it in black and you have an instant aquarium that never needs cleaning.

Sandpaper Surprises—Cover the table with newspaper. Give your child a square of rough grade sandpaper and have them color a design or picture right on it. Do not use words as they will transfer backwards.

Turn the sandpaper face down on a piece of plain paper and cover it with a layer of newspaper. Iron over the top. The iron has to be hot enough to melt the crayons. (AN ADULT SHOULD DO OR CAREFULLY SUPERVISE THIS PROCESS.) After it is cool enough to touch, carefully lift the corner and peel the paper back. The picture should have transferred to the paper.

PAINTING PROJECTS

Cotton Swab Painting—Paint a picture with tempera and cotton swabs. Dip the end of the swab in the paint and place a dot on the paper. Many dots, close together, begin to create the look of point painting used by some master artists, such as Georges Seurat. Continue dots of various colors until your creation is complete.

For variety use a cotton swab dipped in chlorine bleach (ADULT SUPERVISION REQUIRED) and make dots on a piece of very dark blue or black paper. It will bleach the color out so be sure you are working on a pad of newspaper. This makes wonderful snow or nighttime sky designs.

Feather Painting—This technique will give you a whimsical, light look. It is a great way to get the clouds in a bright summer picture. Dip the feather lightly into white paint and stroke lightly across the skyline on blue paper or a blue painted background.

Blow Art—Dribble thin tempera across a piece of paper. Get very close to the paint and blow through a straw to move the paint around and create the look you want.

MORE ART PROJECTS

Art from the Heart!—Children love sending cards to others and what relative or friend would not love receiving a handmade card from your child? Making greeting cards for special occasions allows your child a chance to be creative while also practicing writing skills. Here are steps for making a card with a decorative front cover that resembles rough-textured linen paper.

Materials needed: wax paper, foil, glue, water, facial tissues (white or colored), paintbrush, scissors (decorative ones if possible), a plain sheet of paper

Directions:

1. Cut an 8" x 11" piece of wax paper. Lay it on a foil workspace.

2. Make a glue-water mixture. (About 3 tablespoons white school glue and 3 tablespoons water)

3. Paint the wax paper with glue-water. Then lay the facial tissues on top of the glue. Daub more glue-water onto the tissues. Make it bumpy! Let it dry overnight.

4. Trim the edges.

5. Cut the plain sheet of paper so it is 7" x 10". Write a message on it.

6. Glue the blank side of the plain paper to the wax paper side of the other piece.

7. Fold the card in half. Add decorations if desired.

8. Give your card to someone special!

Styrofoam Tray Prints—Carefully wash meat and vegetable trays when you are finished with them. Trim the edges off so you have a flat piece of styrofoam. Let your child draw a picture on the tray with a sharp pencil. The lines should not cut all the way through, but the indentation needs to be deep enough to make a clear print. Using printers' ink, tempera, or acrylic paint, roll a layer of paint on the tray. You can use an artist brayer, a rolling pin, a pizza roller, or if none of those are available, paint a layer on the tray with a brush. Then turn the tray upside down on a piece of paper and roll over the back of it for an even print. You can use the rollers mentioned above or a large smooth glass or jar. Peel it off carefully and you'll have a perfect print. This process also makes beautiful wrapping paper.

Antique Paper—Using a piece of white paper the size you want for your stationery, create a deckled edge by tearing off the edges all the way around. Paint the paper with a thin coat of tea water. Tea water is made by dissolving 2 tablespoons of instant tea in ¼ cup of water. Leftover brewed tea that has cooled works fine, too. Wash the mixture quickly over the paper being careful not to soak the paper. Lay the stationery between two sheets of waxed paper and cover it with heavy objects until it is dry.

Music Skills Third Graders Need

Music is an important part of the curriculum and our everyday lives. Third graders love singing, tapping, echoing, clapping, moving, listening, plucking, and playing.

TEMPO, DYNAMICS, DURATION, AND TONE

* Identify the speed of the beat: slow, fast, getting slower, getting faster

* Use tempo to express different styles

* Distinguish between soft, very soft, loud, and very loud tones

* Associate those with music terms: piano (p), pianissimo (pp), forte (f), fortissimo (ff)

* Sing or play an instrument to demonstrate these terms

* Demonstrate an understanding of meter, rhythm, and length of notes

* Identify and respond to musical symbols

* Practice singing or playing a scale up and down

FORM AND STYLE

* Identify, reproduce, and create verse and refrain patterns

* Recognize and sing or move to a variety of musical styles from various cultures

* Recognize and sing rounds

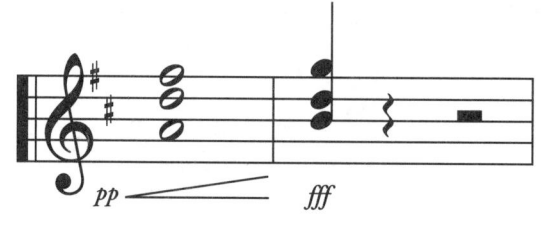

MUSIC APPRECIATION

* Respond to and enjoy a variety of music

* Identify instruments and their "families"

* Become aware of the works of great composers and musicians

* Recognize the qualities of good singing

* Participate in musical activities

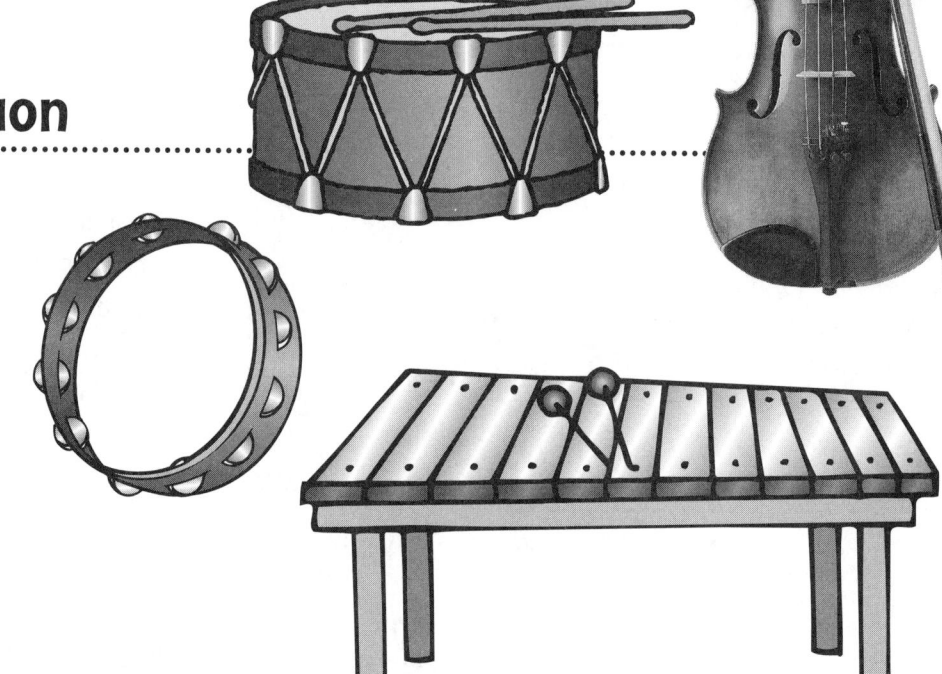

MAKE MUSICAL MAGIC WITH YOUR CHILD!

Draw What You Hear— Respond to music with your child. Share a giant piece of paper and some crayons. As you both listen to some interesting music, just let the crayons flow down the paper. When the song is completed, talk about what you felt when you made certain designs on the picture.

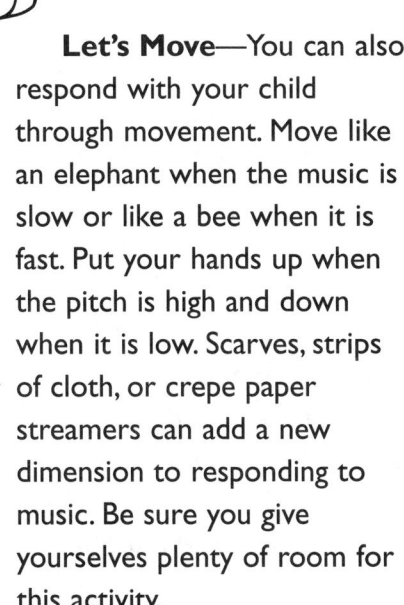

For a variation on this activity, decide before you listen, how to respond to a certain tempo or pitch. Perhaps you want to use dots when the tempo is fast and lines when the music slows. Perhaps you want to use circles when the pitch is low and triangles when the pitch is high. When the song is finished, take a look at your artistic response to that music.

Let's Move—You can also respond with your child through movement. Move like an elephant when the music is slow or like a bee when it is fast. Put your hands up when the pitch is high and down when it is low. Scarves, strips of cloth, or crepe paper streamers can add a new dimension to responding to music. Be sure you give yourselves plenty of room for this activity.

Rewrite It—Make up new words to old tunes. For example, instead of "Mary Had a Little Lamb" perhaps "Mary Had a Loaf of Bread!" Some of the lyrics will get silly and giggles will result from this fun activity. This is a great game to play while riding in the car. It is also good to connect the lyrics to a topic your child is studying at school.

Echo Sing—Echo singing results when one partner sings a line and the other sings it back. You don't have to be a great singer to enjoy this with your child. Just make your voice use different pitches, rhythms, and tempos to make your child aware of the variety.

Whose Voice?—Use different voices. First sing an old familiar song like "Here We Go 'Round the Mulberry Bush" in your regular voice. Next sing it in a very deep voice like a dinosaur might have sung it. Then try it the way a tiny fairy might sing it using a high pitched voice. Have fun by wiggling your index finger quickly between your lips as you sing like a goldfish underwater!

MUSICAL INSTRUMENTS

Water Xylophone—Fill glass jars or drinking glasses with various amounts of water to make a xylophone. Fill the first jar with a tiny amount of water, the next with a bit more, and so on until the final glass is nearly full. Using eight glasses allows you to replicate the scale. Let your child use a wooden spoon handle, dowel, or pencil to tap each glass and create melodies.

You can make a variation of this instrument using small-mouth glass bottles. Rather than striking the bottles, have your child blow across the top of each, experimenting until a position is found that makes a rich sound.

Coffee Can Drum—Cut both ends out of any size coffee can and cover them with the can's plastic lids. (One lid will have to be saved from a previous can.) If you want, tie a cord around the center of the drum, making it long enough to go around your child's neck so the drum will hang down. Let your child use wooden spoon handles, dowels, or pencils as drumsticks and beat out a rhythm. You can use oatmeal boxes or tubes in place of the can. Cover the ends with rubber sheeting, vinyl, self-adhesive paper, or large balloons. Use large rubber bands to hold the sheeting and vinyl in place. Let your child decorate the drum with wallpaper, gift wrap, or paint.

Comb Flute—Fold a piece of plain paper over the teeth edge of a short, clean comb. Hold it between your lips and hum out a tune. How can you make it sound louder? How can you make the pitch higher? Can you play a favorite tune?

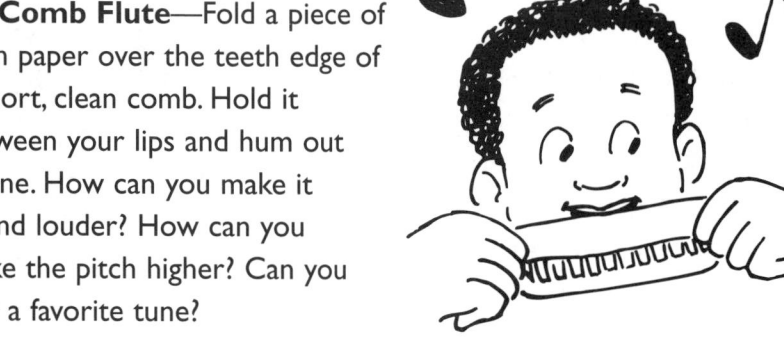

Light Bulb Maracas—Make your own maracas! You will need two used light bulbs, lots of inch-wide strips of newspaper, and a paste made from flour mixed with water. Cover your work area as this is messy! Let your child begin dipping the strips in the paste. Slide the strips between two fingers to strip off excess paste and drape them onto the light bulbs.

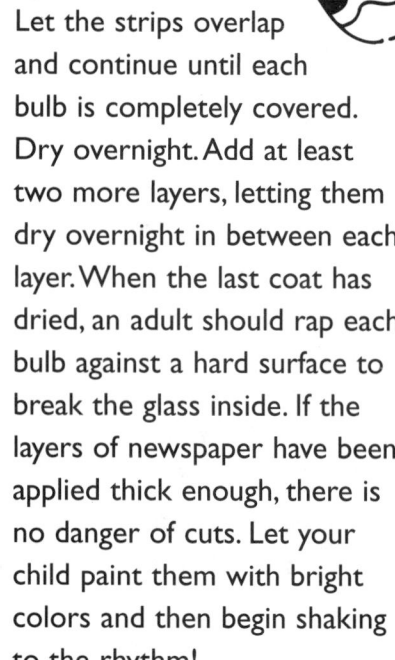

Let the strips overlap and continue until each bulb is completely covered. Dry overnight. Add at least two more layers, letting them dry overnight in between each layer. When the last coat has dried, an adult should rap each bulb against a hard surface to break the glass inside. If the layers of newspaper have been applied thick enough, there is no danger of cuts. Let your child paint them with bright colors and then begin shaking to the rhythm!

Physical Education Skills Third Graders Need

Physical fitness is one key to a healthy, balanced life. Physical education gives children a chance to learn about their bodies through sports and games. Physical education focuses on strength, balance, flexibility, and endurance. Third graders usually learn the skills required to play popular sports, but most games are simplified, less competitive versions. The other key component of physical education is learning to play and work together.

PRESIDENT'S COUNCIL ON PHYSICAL FITNESS

These are the activities established by the President's Council to demonstrate fitness. The requirements vary by age and sex.

* Curl ups
* Shuttle run
* Sit and reach
* One mile run/walk
* Pull-ups
* Flexed-arm hang

FAMILY FITNESS FUN

Family fitness fun should just be a part of your everyday lives. Modeling good wellness routines important to you and adding fitness in a fun way is the perfect addition to that philosophy.

* Whenever possible, walk or ride bikes instead of driving to school, the library, the store, or a park.

* Get the whole family involved in a team sport like softball or basketball.

* If your child has a special sports interest try to become actively involved or at least become knowledgeable of the rules. Your child will feel supported and valued because of your interest.

* Try to spend at least half an hour outside with your child each day. Perhaps you can play catch, fly a kite, or just go for a walk.

* Involve your child as much as you can in sports you enjoy. Create awareness in your child for lifetime leisure time activities.

FITNESS AND ATTITUDE

* Cross the horizontal ladder
* Jog for five minutes
* Jump rope for endurance
* Bounce, throw, and catch a ball
* Perform warm-up exercises
* Perform simple rhythmic activities
* Accept responsibilities as a team player
* Demonstrate good sportsmanship
* Participate safely
* Give top effort
* Play fair
* Take care of equipment
* Respect other students and teachers
* Follow directions

PHYSICAL FITNESS FUN!

Jump the Ball!—You will need a ball attached to a nine-foot-long rope. (A punch ball which you can buy at discount stores works great.) One person stands in the middle and twirls the ball around in a circle. Be sure the ball just skims the top of the ground or floor. The other person stands about nine feet away. As the ball

comes around, the outside person attempts to jump over the ball without being touched. If the ball is touched at all, the two trade places. The spinner can increase or decrease the speed of the ball to trick the jumper.

Stop the Ball!—This is a variation of the above game. One person sits down on the perimeter of the circle while the other person spins the

ball. The object is to flick your feet out and stop the ball as it passes by.

Balloon Walk—This game is more fun and more challenging with a lot of players. For best results, play on a hard surface area. Tie a balloon with a cord or strong ribbon to the ankle of every player. The object is to break the balloon on the other players' legs without allowing your own balloon to be broken!

Keep it up!—Blow up an extra large balloon. Toss it up in the air and bounce it back and forth, trying to keep it from touching the ground. A player who allows it to touch the ground gets a penalty letter. The letters should spell out " b-a-l-l-o-o-n". If you are the first to spell the whole word, the other player wins. You can play this game with a group. Each player is eliminated as they spell "balloon." The last player left in the game is the winner.

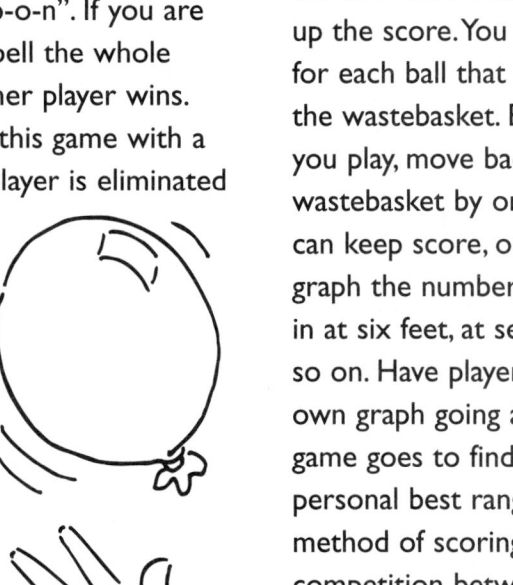

Indoor Hoops—Create safe balls out of wadded up newspaper wrapped with masking tape. Each player should have four of them. Write the players' initials on all of their balls. Set an empty wastebasket a certain distance away depending upon your child's ability to throw and mastery of eye-hand coordination. At a signal, both players start throwing the balls toward the wastebasket. Only one throw per ball. When all the balls have been tossed, add up the score. You get one point for each ball that landed inside the wastebasket. Each round you play, move back from the wastebasket by one foot. You can keep score, or you can graph the number player A got in at six feet, at seven feet, and so on. Have players keep their own graph going as far as the game goes to find their personal best range. The latter method of scoring eliminates competition between players and focuses on improving your own personal skills.

MORE PHYSICAL FUN!

Rainbow Twist—Tape sheets of five or more colors of paper to the floor. For each sheet, place a small matching scrap of paper in a box. Call out a body part and draw a color from the box. Ask your child to place that body part on the matching color sheet.

Examples: Put your left arm on black; put your head on red. This game is a fun one to play in your stocking feet. Be prepared for lots of giggles. Be sure to take a turn yourself!

Mirror, Mirror on the Wall—Play "mirror" with your child by facing each other either standing or sitting. Move your left arm very slowly and watch your child move the right arm to match the "mirror image." Then it's your child's turn.

Follow each movement carefully and slowly. This is a wonderful relaxing, quiet activity that can create a calm time in the midst of a hectic day.

Nature Imitation—Call out an animal name and see if you and your child can imitate the way the animal moves. Try caterpillar, elephant, snake, bee, and kangaroo for starters! Take turns naming the animal.

Bean Bag Throw—Set up targets in your yard or at a park. See if your child can throw a bean bag that lands right on the target. If you don't have bean bags, you can make some inexpensive ones by buying a bag of dry beans and then putting them in zip-shut sandwich bags. Put the beans in one bag until it is about two-thirds full. Zip it shut after you squeeze all the air out. Then put that bag into another zip-shut bag with the first one turned upside down. Toss it

like a regular bean bag. Check it often for rips and just add another bag.

Another inexpensive bean bag can be made by filling the bottom of an old sock with beans and sewing the top shut. Cut the sock off at the ankle and use the foot part. Make sure there are no holes in the sock and check the stitching after several uses.

Toss it up!—You will need a small tablecloth or square of material and a ball or balloon. Your child needs to hold two corners and you hold two corners tightly. Try moving the ball around on the cloth and tossing it up in the air. This is fun to do while exciting march music is playing in the background. It encourages cooperation among the players to keep the ball on the cloth.

Social Skills Third Graders Need

Although academics are the main thrust of your child's education, he or she cannot succeed at school without some basic social skills. This next section will address several key areas, including respect, responsibility, classroom interactions, problems with peers, manners, and safety issues.

RESPECT FOR OTHERS

Listen—Discuss with your child the importance and benefits of listening to others and their opinions. You can explain that everyone has differences of opinions and everyone has the right to express those opinions. Even if you don't agree with others' ideas, you still need to

> The Golden Rule— "Treat others as you would like them to treat you" is the foundation of working, playing, and getting along with others. Your home is the place your child should first learn and practice the Golden Rule, then he or she will be able to apply it to peer, school, and community situations.

respectfully listen, and then you can have the opportunity to express your point of view. Demonstrate your respect for your child by listening to his or her opinions. This provides an excellent model through which your child can see how important it is to respect other people.

Cultural Diversity—Third graders are ready to appreciate the diversity of people and are alert to likenesses and differences. Encourage your child to ask questions and explore ethnic diversity in your community. Invite guests from other cultures or lands to share their customs if you have the opportunity. Cook foreign dishes on occasion or dine at ethnic restaurants and bazaars to sample foods of different cultures. Speak positively of the contributions of people from many backgrounds.

RESPECT FOR ONESELF

Third graders are already aware of the times when they do their best work. They are proud of those efforts and excited to share their feelings with adults. The attention you are paying through daily interactions will allow your child to feel safe, secure, and worthy. A child with a sense of self-worth will demonstrate it by standing up for himself or herself and for the ideals parents have nurtured. This same child will be less likely to be coaxed or lured into dangerous or destructive situations. He or she has the confidence to express and pursue goals, to withstand peer pressures better, and to explore new horizons. Encourage your child to be his or her own best friend!

We're Proud of You—Recognize your child's strengths and "broadcast" those abilities. You don't need to report it on the national news, but display it proudly where your child can see it every day. Set up a bulletin board or an area on the refrigerator for each of your children. Exhibit good schoolwork, proud photos, notes of love and praise, and special awards. Be creative and proud!

RESPECT FOR AUTHORITY

People—The teachers, principal, secretaries, and other support staff who work at your child's school are there because they care about children. Teach your child that those people are responsible for the safety and success of the school and they can't do their jobs without respect from all members of the school community. Discuss examples of showing respect for authority, such as speaking in a considerate manner and following directions.

School Rules

* Use an appropriate voice.

* Give your best effort.

* Use your time wisely.

* Ask questions if you don't understand.

* Respect the thoughts and feelings of others.

* Be responsible and dependable.

* Participate in all activities.

* Work and play safely.

* Take care of school property.

Rules

Get a copy of your child's school handbook and ask the teacher for a list of rules that are established for the classroom. Some typical ones are noted in the gray box on the left.

Discuss the rules with your child. Be sure he or she understands not only the rule, but the reason for the rule.

If any of the school's rules conflict with your household rules, discuss them with your child. Help your child understand the importance of following the rules for whatever community he or she is visiting—school, a friend's home, another country. If there is a school rule that strongly contradicts your personal or religious beliefs, speak with your child's teacher. Many times an alternative can be agreed to that achieves the same goal and respects the rights of all.

RESPECT FOR PROPERTY

* Discuss the many ways we care for property, such as putting things back where they belong, asking before borrowing, using equipment properly, or picking up litter on the playground.

* As you drive past an example of vandalism or graffiti, point it out to your child. Explain the destructiveness of such acts. Emphasize the lack of respect they demonstrate. Help your child empathize with the people who have to clean up, fix, or replace the damaged property. Follow up with information regarding the

> Children need to take care of their own property and that of the school. They also need to respect the things that belong to their classmates.

punishments for such behavior. Remind your child that all choices have consequences.

RESPONSIBILITY

Your child needs to be independent in applying learning strategies and able to be relied upon by you to complete a task. A child who is dependent on the parent for decision making and goal setting is handicapped for life.

✳ The most basic way to teach your child responsibility is through chores. Hold a family meeting and together make a list of the things that need to get done in order for the family to live in a clean, safe, and healthy home. Let family members first sign up for daily and weekly chores they want to do. Then see what's left! Encourage everyone to be involved in a fair solution for dividing and assigning the remaining chores. Set guidelines for when chores need to be finished. Then let children take responsibility for doing them or losing the privilege of playing or participating in extra-curricular activities.

✳ Arrange situations where your child can make important choices. It could be as simple as, "We need one dozen doughnuts. Please choose an

wash dishes
bathe dog
water plants

assortment for us." Of course, when you allow your child to make choices you must accept that decision without redirection, so choose the situation carefully.

✳ Occasionally a child who is allowed to make choices and decisions that are important will assume that family or parent decisions are now under his or her control. You can manage this situation by explaining that some choices belong to third graders and some choices belong to adults.

✳ Assist your child in becoming responsible by establishing a location by the door or on a special shelf where lunch money, library books, permission slips, and homework should always be placed. This spot should be easily accessible to your child. Reinforce the use of this collection spot until it becomes a habit for your child. Point out how much smoother the morning goes when everything that is needed for the day is in one location.

Your child will be responsible for his or her actions or assignments only if you do not take the responsibility for those tasks yourself.

✳ When your child makes a choice to be involved in an activity, such as a class play, piano lessons, or soccer team, it is important to stress the commitment of that decision. Responsible adults learned in their early years that once you have dedicated your efforts, completing the task or event is vital. Stress the fact that others are depending on each individual in order for the event to be successful.

✳ All of us fail to be reliable or dependable at some time when we forget or avoid a task. Be understanding. Teach your child that if an effort to be reliable fails, the best policy is to be honest and not to blame others for your failure. If your child forgets lunch money, he or she should tell the teacher. If your child ran out of time to finish the homework, he or she should write the note explaining why. If your child forgot to walk the dog, the child should be honest and tell the adult involved.

CLASSROOM INTERACTIONS

A Wide Range of Students—Children come in all shapes, sizes, and abilities and all have their own strengths and weaknesses. Your child needs to know how to interact with children who may be quicker or slower, rude or considerate, shy or bossy, physically challenged or athletic, or many other combinations.

Help your child be aware of the uniqueness of each classmate and how important each one is to the class. Encourage your child to write a kind note to a classmate or to pass on compliments periodically. Everyone likes to be appreciated!

Act out "pretend" situations that might occur in the classroom. This will help your child be prepared to meet those challenging times. For example, if another child is coaxing your child to refuse to play with a handicapped classmate, you could be your child and demonstrate exactly what you would say and do to stand up for the classmate who is being excluded. Your child could "play" the part of the "ring-leader" and try to get you to cooperate in the conspiracy. Later your child could "play" the part of the handicapped friend so that the feelings of being ignored could be explored. Scenarios like this could come right from after-school conversations that clue you in on what is worrying your child.

> **Group members**
> - listen
> - give ideas
> - take turns
> - work hard even if their idea wasn't chosen

Cooperative Groups—Being able to work with a partner, a small group, or the entire class, is an important part of your child's learning. Ask your child which activities he or she likes to do alone and which with a group. Talk about reasons your child likes or dislikes solitary or group activities.

If your child has trouble working in groups, you can help your child by comparing learning groups to your family. Everyone has certain jobs to do so that all the work gets done. Then everyone benefits by getting to do fun things together. Encourage your child to be a team player. Make a list of what things individuals need to do in order for the group to succeed. Have your child identify areas where he or she and other group members need to improve.

Asking for Help

If your child indicates confusion about assignments, find out if he or she asks the teacher for help when needed. Try to determine why your child doesn't understand something. Write a note or call the teacher if your child indicates further lack of understanding or a fear of asking for help.

PROBLEMS WITH PALS

Too Shy/Too Aggressive—If your child is too shy or too aggressive to make and keep friends, you can help make a list of things good friends do. Your child may list these items: sharing, doing things  together, taking turns, being kind to each other, or sticking together. Point out some of these traits that your child could work on to become a better friend. It may also be helpful to find another child in the class who experiences the same character trait. For example, two shy people might play and work well together because they won't feel dominated. Conversely, if two aggressive kids pair up, they may learn what it's like for others when trying to work or play with someone who always has to get his or her own way.

Bullies—If your child is being picked on, the teacher should be made aware of the situation. Confident children have less trouble with harassment and bullies at school. If your child experiences these problems, schedule a conference with the teacher and determine if staff members are witnessing the same problem. Work together with your child and the teacher to select a course of action. Continually express to your child that you are sure he or she can handle the problem and that you are there for support.

Suggest a silent signal that could be shown to a teacher to indicate the problem. Perhaps your child could choose to play or work with other children at a different location.

Being Excluded—If your child is feeling excluded, be sure the teacher is aware of the concern. Perhaps the teacher can offer another point of view or can visit with the classmate(s) whose behavior is making your child uncomfortable. It may simply be an overstatement of a situation by your child and the teacher can be alert to times when your child is included and participating readily. Sometimes just pointing out these positive experiences will allow the third grader to realize that things aren't all that bad. However, if there really is a problem, the teacher needs to be aware of the hurt feelings that are being experienced. An adult can often suggest simple all-inclusion tactics to eliminate the problem such as, "I see your team needs another player. Sam's ready to go!"

At home, you might arrange a situation where the classmate who is excluding your child could be involved with a family activity or be invited to come over to play after school. Be sure your child is in agreement with this idea and be sure that you will be able to be a part of the activity. Use the time as a positive experience for both children, and eliminate any criticisms. As the time together progresses, you can evaluate the possibility of repeating the invitation or involving more children next time. Let your child be a part of the decision regarding that next step.

PROBLEM SOLVING

Every journey through life includes a few bumps. And some children and adults will experience several! You can help your child by leading him or her through a process to try whenever a problem arises.

Use the picture below to "walk" your child through the "steps" of problem solving. It might be helpful to copy this chart and actually write out some of the steps with your child. This process should be completed using several different types of problems, including a behavioral concern, a science experiment, or a mathematical problem. The benefit for your child will come in repeating the process. It allows him or her to approach a problem with a logical thought process instead of reacting without thinking things through.

The best way to demonstrate how well this works is for you to apply it to a simple problem you are trying to solve at home. Talk it through out loud with your child and explain each level of the procedure as you go. Celebrate the results when it is completed, or point out that it may be necessary to repeat some steps to solve the problem.

Fairness is an important concern, especially for children. If your child is considering ideas for solving a behavioral or social problem, ask him or her to evaluate whether each solution is a "fair" one.

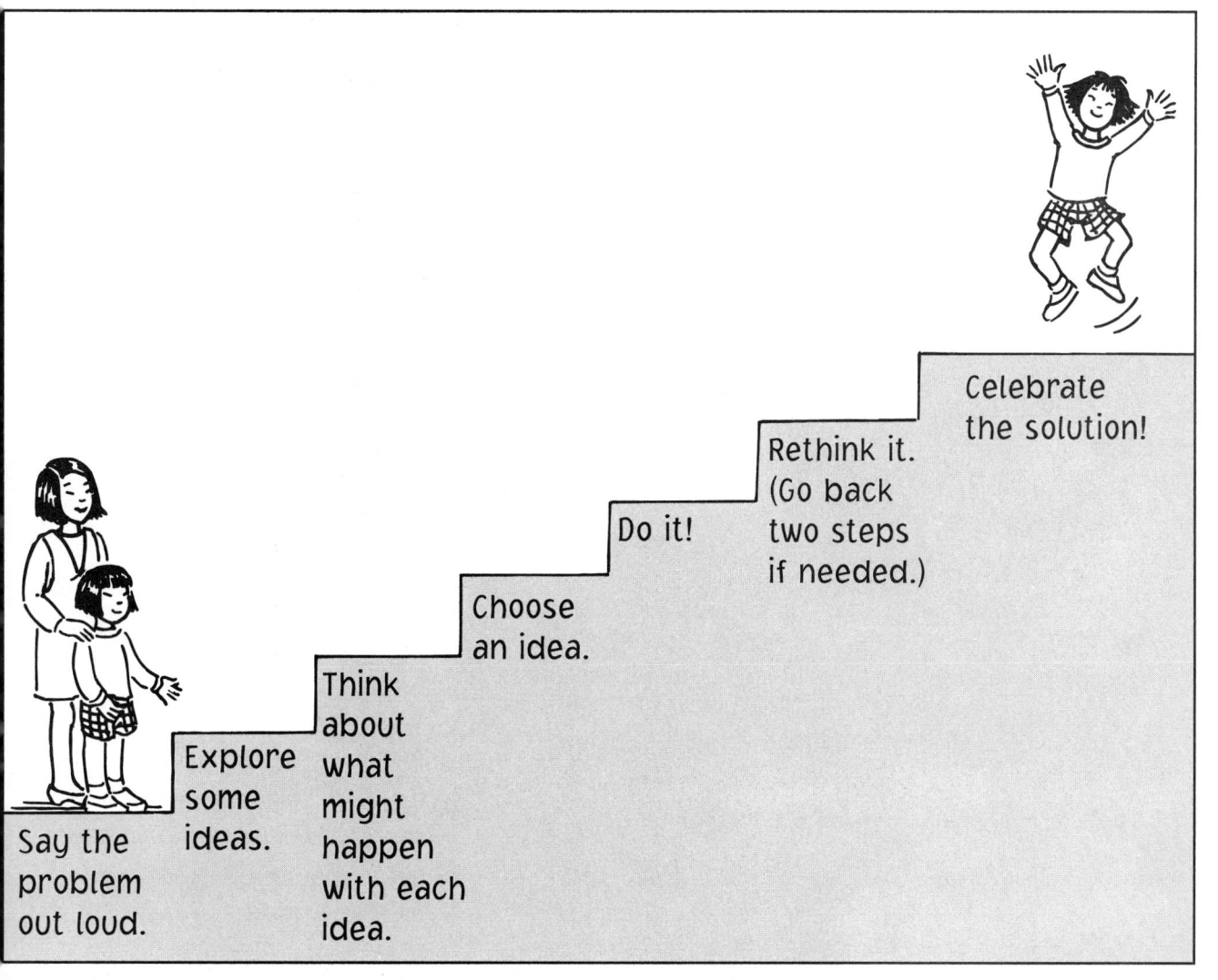

Say the problem out loud.

Explore some ideas.

Think about what might happen with each idea.

Choose an idea.

Do it!

Rethink it. (Go back two steps if needed.)

Celebrate the solution!

MANNERLY MOVES

One of the best ways for your child to find acceptance and friendship, wherever he or she goes, is to exhibit good manners. Politeness is rewarded in all areas of society and will help your child succeed in situations with other children and adults.

Manners do not have to be taught in isolation. They are more quickly mastered and remembered by practicing on a daily basis. Perhaps most important is for adults to use good manners, especially when dealing with children.

At School

* **Classroom**—Sharing the teacher's attention is vital since all the children deserve a turn. Remind your child how important it is to raise hands and wait for a turn to speak so that others can hear each great idea.

* **Cafeteria**—Standing in line, waiting for one's turn, saying *please* and *thank you*, using good table manners, chewing with one's mouth closed, and talking quietly will help your child enjoy the noon meal with friends.

* **Playground**—Good manners on the playground will eliminate arguments and hurt feelings, and provide for a safe playtime. Encourage your child to take turns on the slide and wait patiently for the tether ball. Sharing the ball with others and complimenting great effort by friends will make recess more enjoyable for all.

There is rarely a time in school when sharing and cooperation are not involved in the situation. Helping your child to be an expert at these skills will make the school day more beneficial and productive.

At Home

Practice using *please* and *thank you* with family members. Another term children should learn is *Pardon?* when they don't hear or understand something, instead of *What?* or *Huh?* The more habitual it becomes, the easier it is. Using good manners will also demonstrate respect and love for each other and will lead to more pleasant family times.

Interruptions into other people's conversations should be minimal since the polite move would be to wait patiently for a turn to speak. However, when interruptions are unavoidable, teach your child to say, "Excuse me." You can then expand that to other situations where it is applicable, such as crossing in front of someone or stepping on another person's foot.

One fun way to practice manners is on the telephone. Role play the polite way to answer the phone and take messages.

(You may also want to introduce how to safely respond if a child is home alone without a parent. *My mom can't come to the phone right now. May I take a message?*)

SAFETY CONCERNS

Traveling To and From School—Review the process of getting to and from school each year with your child. Before the new term starts, walk or ride the route as a family if your child walks or rides a bike. Point out any dangerous intersections. Remind your child to cross only at marked areas and to obey any crossing guards. Stress the importance of following the safe, direct route every day.

If your child is riding on a bus to school, practice getting to the bus stop on time. Explain that the bus driver's directions must be followed for safety. Children should be taught to stay seated, talk quietly, and not bother others on the bus.

Home Alone—If your child must be home alone at any time, it is vital that safety rules be written down and practiced. Let your child be involved in establishing the rules for this time. Perhaps your child needs to call you at the office upon arriving home. Be sure the office number and any emergency numbers are posted by the phone. Clearly define rules about what food is permissible to eat, when friends can be invited over, what chores need to be accomplished, and what leisure activities are acceptable.

Fire Safety—Your child will practice fire drills periodically at school and you can reinforce this with family fire drills at home.

✱ Review procedures for getting out of the building. Find and practice alternate escape routes. Choose a place outside away from your home to meet.

✱ Make sure your child knows to *Stop, drop, and roll* if clothing catches on fire.

✱ Teach your child to crawl to safety if there is heavy smoke. (The air is cooler and cleaner near the floor.)

Safety is an important social issue because children need to look out for themselves and those around them. The best bet for safety is preparedness. Should an emergency occur, it is comforting to know that you did everything you could to prepare your child for it.

Your child will be excited to report to the class that your family is well prepared.

Stranger Safety—In today's society, it is critical that your child understand the dangers of talking to strangers. Start by explaining that a stranger is anyone your child doesn't know, even if that person claims to know him or her. Act out some scenarios that may occur or that you have read about in the newspaper and see if your child is prepared to refuse any advances of a stranger. Especially instruct your child never to enter a stranger's vehicle, and never to open the door to a stranger or let anyone in the house without permission. Teach your child to yell and run if approached by a stranger.

Home and School Cooperation

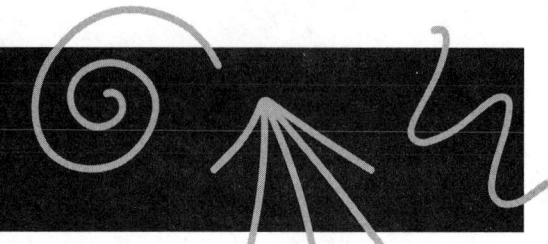

COMMUNICATING WITH YOUR CHILD'S TEACHER

Because time is so limited in everyone's busy schedule, communication is often short and single-focused. Everyone experiences the same time restraints and the frustration it causes. For that reason, when you need to contact your child's teacher, be specific and considerate of the school schedule.

✳ Contact the teacher with positive comments as well as concerns.

✳ Keep the conversation on topic. Discuss only the essentials.

✳ Try to share concerns and suggestions as efficiently as possible.

✳ Offer to help solve a problem or concern. Make suggestions carefully so as not to indicate concern about the teacher's ability to handle it.

✳ Keep conversations with the teacher confidential especially if other students are involved.

✳ If you have a request, make it in writing by sending a note with your child.

✳ Keep a sense of humor about classroom situations and share it with the teacher.

✳ Respond to class projects by sending a note or making a phone call to express your pride at your child's work.

✳ If you offer to help in the classroom, be prompt.

✳ Offer curriculum support with materials or resource people.

COMMUNICATING WITH YOUR CHILD'S SCHOOL ADMINISTRATOR

✳ When you see or hear about something positive and exciting happening at the school, call the administrator or send a note.

✳ If you have a question about the reason for a school rule, contact the administrator with that question. Approach it with curiosity or concern, not animosity.

✳ If disagreements arise, explain your viewpoint calmly and have a reason for your opinion.

✳ Participate in parent groups by attending meetings and volunteering whenever possible.

✳ Attend board meetings to become better informed about school policy.

TOP TEN WAYS FOR COMMUNICATING WITH YOUR CHILD

1 Focus on the relationship with your child. Demonstrate your love every day! A child who experiences love flourishes in all aspects of life.

2 Listen to your child. Even though the topic may not interest you, pay attention.

3 Model patience and teach it. Then when you are busy and ask your child to be patient and wait, he or she will believe you. When you ask for patience, you will need to insist on it and not give in or become irritated.

4 Be ready to admit that you are not perfect! Recognize that you will make mistakes and talk to your child about it. Show him or her that mistakes or failures are a part of the learning process. Don't hesitate to admit you don't know something. Just be ready to find out.

5 Encourage independence. Over-protection handicaps children in every avenue of life. You certainly want your child to have roots, but you must also be ready to offer wings to fly, explore, and make his or her own mistakes.

6 Maintain a sense of humor. Accidents will happen. Plans will fall apart. Try to laugh at yourself and at the quirks in everyday life.

7 Set guidelines and stick to them. Consistency is very important as it provides children with stability in their lives. Children need and want lines of behavior drawn and they need to know that those don't change with the whims of the day. Discipline should be directed at the act, not the child.

8 Stay focused on the long-term goal of raising a happy, healthy child who will contribute in a positive way to society. Many pitfalls will occur along the way. Try not to worry about the minor events.

9 Spend time with your child. Include your child in your activities and get involved in the things that interest him or her. The quantity of time is important, but it's the quality of that time that reaps great rewards.

10 Most important of all, practice what you preach. If you want your child to respect and uphold your examples and decisions, then follow the same rules of respect and responsibility that you teach.

CREATING COOPERATIVE CONFERENCES

Conferences come in all shapes and sizes! Some may be formally planned and scheduled. Others may be impromptu and informal. Some may include several people who work with the child. Some may include only the teacher and you. Others may include your child. You and the classroom teacher generally make the decisions as to how a conference is to be organized. Once that is established, the important goal is to make that conference productive for your child's learning process.

The teacher will come with documentation and observations of how your child functions in the classroom. It is like the teacher has a photograph in his or her mind of your child as a classroom learner.

You should also come with ideas and information about how your child functions at home. It is like you have a photograph in your mind of how your child learns at home.

My child learns best by . . .

My child worries about . . .

My child likes . . .

My child does not like . . .

My child is confused about . . .

The object is to combine those two photographs into a picture that is more nearly what your child is truly like.

You and the teacher will share ideas each work with your child in each setting. You will share strengths, abilities, gifts, and areas that need improvement. The sharing that occurs at a conference of any type is what will create a better situation for your child.

Here are some conference tips:

* If you don't understand something the teacher said, ask for it to be repeated and explained.

* Be sure you stay focused on the topic of the conference which is your child, not your neighbor's child.

* Don't schedule a conference if you are angry. Get your emotions in check first and then approach in a rational way.

* Use phrases like "Can you tell me more about that situation?"

* Bring these notes with you:

I had a question about
_____

I am confused about
_____

I really like
_____

I wanted you to know that
_____

VOLUNTEERING

There are many benefits to being an involved parent:

* Your child is proud of your help and knows you support the school and its educational activities

* You learn how the class operates and the expectations the teacher holds

* You meet the children your child interacts with

* You are more aware of classroom topics and schoolwide concerns

* The teacher knows you care and thinks of your child every time he or she sees you

Here are some ways your help would really HELP!

Most teachers encourage parents to become involved at school. They will appreciate any assistance you can give whether it is a one-time special event or help on a regular basis.

At school, working with children:

* Listen to children read

* Do flashcard drills

* Help with creative writing

* Assist in the computer lab

* Give a book talk on a children's book you read

* Share a special talent or hobby

* Work with a small group for a short-term project—science fair, book discussion groups, etc.

At home:

* Type or do word processing

* Write notes or letters

* Translate forms

* Tape-record books for listening libraries

* Prepare snacks

* Plan holiday celebrations

* Recruit resource people

Volunteers Are Great!

Good with children

Ready on time

Enormously important

Appreciated by all

Truly make a difference!

At school, working without children:

* Put up bulletin boards

* Maintain the classroom or school library

* Prepare materials for lessons

* File student work

* Cut out and laminate materials

* Assemble packets for the school

* Work a shift at special events—book fair, auction, carnival, garage sale, etc.

HOMEWORK

Have you ever tried to bake a cake and discovered you had no flour? It requires a quick trip to the store. When you return, you find that the pan is dirty and has to be washed. Then you can't find a rubber scraper to clean the bowl. By the time you get the cake done, you are totally frustrated.

Your child will feel the same way if you expect him or her to complete homework without the right tools. Assemble the items listed in the box on the right. Then create a workspace where everything is organized and ready to use.

Above the workspace, which could be a desk or table top, hang a bulletin board or spare ceiling tiles. Your child can pin notes, a calendar, and a schedule up there for easy reference.

In this book you will find many notes or guides that would be good to display at your child's workspace:

* SEARCH cue card (page 7)

* SCOPE editing tips (page 16)

* spelling procedure (page 19)

* penmanship guides (pages 21–22)

* math problem-solving strategies (page 30)

Encourage your child to make a schedule each night. Have your child use page 94 and jot down what homework has been assigned and mark what needs to be done first. Some children like to do the hard tasks first, others like to get the easy ones done first. Let your child choose, and then check to see if the schedule plan is working.

Homework Supplies

* Variety of types of paper including plain, lined, and colored paper

* Scrap paper to be used for notes (Recycle the backs of used sheets, mail that came with nothing on the back, or mistakes from the computer printer.)

* Pens and pencils (Be sure the pens have ink and the pencils have points.)

* Pencil sharpener

* Erasers—either a large art one or ones on the ends of pencils

* Ruler—one with both metric and customary markings

* Scissors

* Crayons and markers

* Glue, paste, or rubber cement

* Dictionary

* Atlas or globe

Bookmarks

YOU really hopped to it!

"Every bunny" is proud of you!

Here's the scoop...

Your work has been terrific!

You have many gifts!

But the best gift of all...

is YOU!

YOU are on the ROAD to SUCCESS!

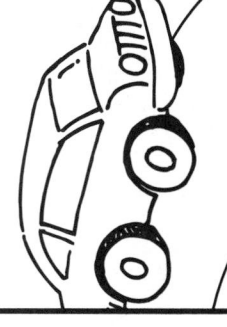

CELEBRATE! You should be very proud!

Backs of Bookmark Rewards

 • FS-23004 Skills for Success for Your Third Grader • © Frank Schaffer Publications, Inc.

"Bee" a Great Reader!

Do this page after you read a story.
Read each question.
Color its honeycomb section if you can answer it.

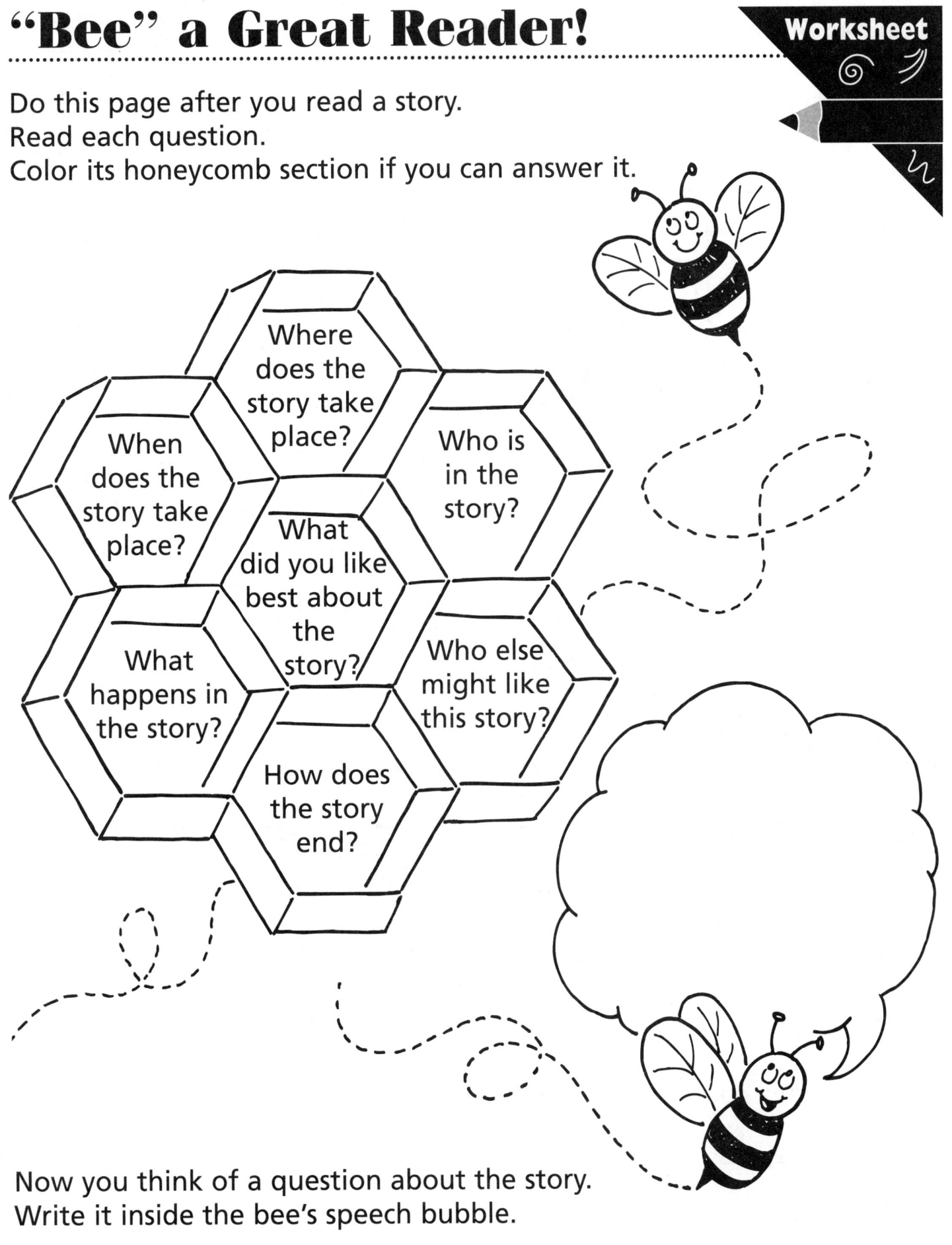

When does the story take place?

Where does the story take place?

Who is in the story?

What did you like best about the story?

What happens in the story?

Who else might like this story?

How does the story end?

Now you think of a question about the story.
Write it inside the bee's speech bubble.

Contraction Convoy

Make a contraction from the words on the wheels of each truck. Write it on the truck.

Read each contraction.
On the wheels, write the two words it is made from.

Write as many contractions as you can that have the word **not** in them.

_____

_____

Vowels in Bloom

Look at the word in each flower. Choose words from the watering can that have the same vowel combination.
Write them on the leaves.

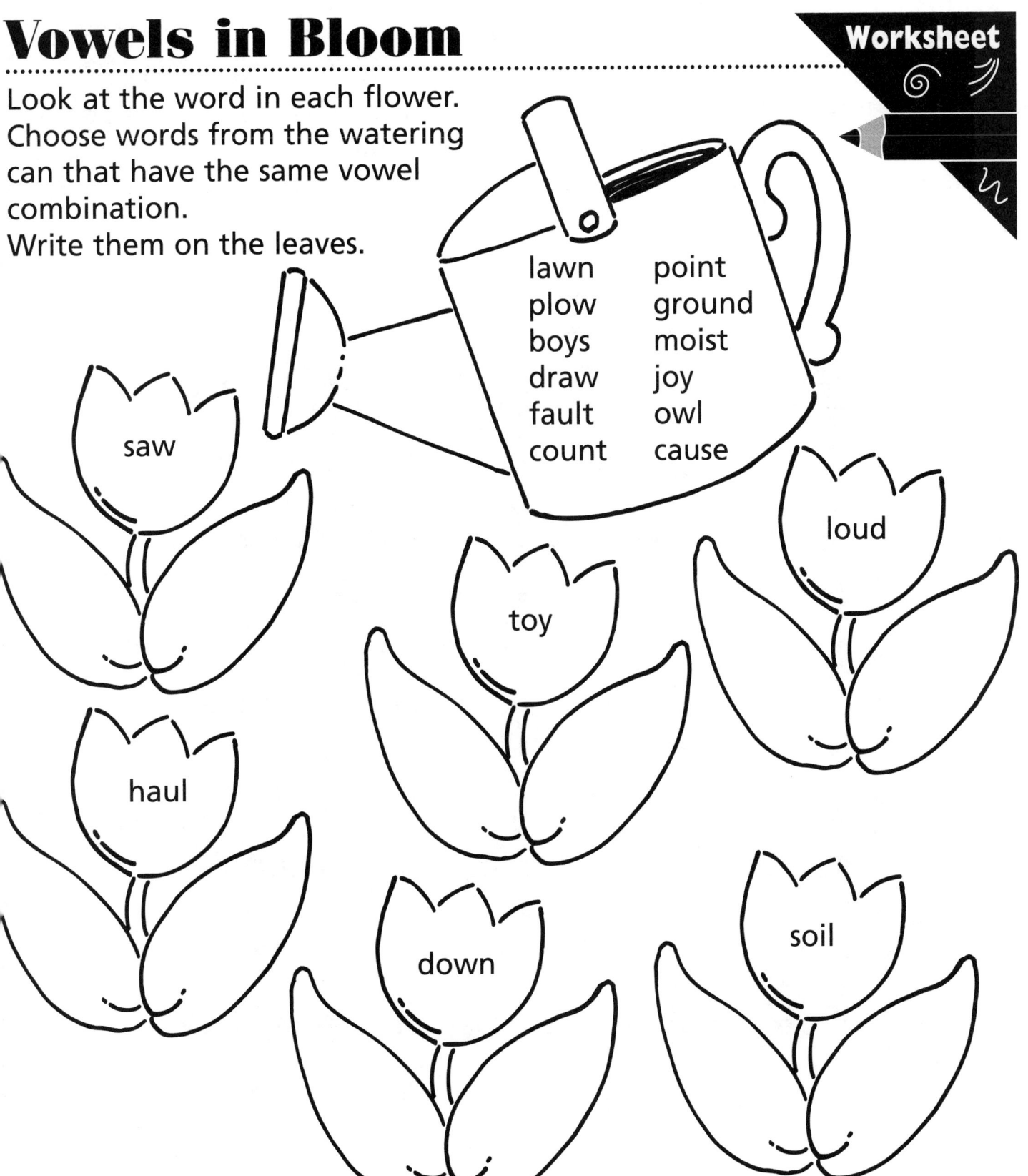

lawn   point
plow   ground
boys   moist
draw   joy
fault   owl
count cause

saw

loud

toy

haul

down

soil

Think of other words that have those vowel combinations. Write three.

Checkerboard Match-up!

Place one index finger on a checker and your other index finger on a square. Do they make a word? Some checkers may work in more than one place. Can you make more than 30 words?

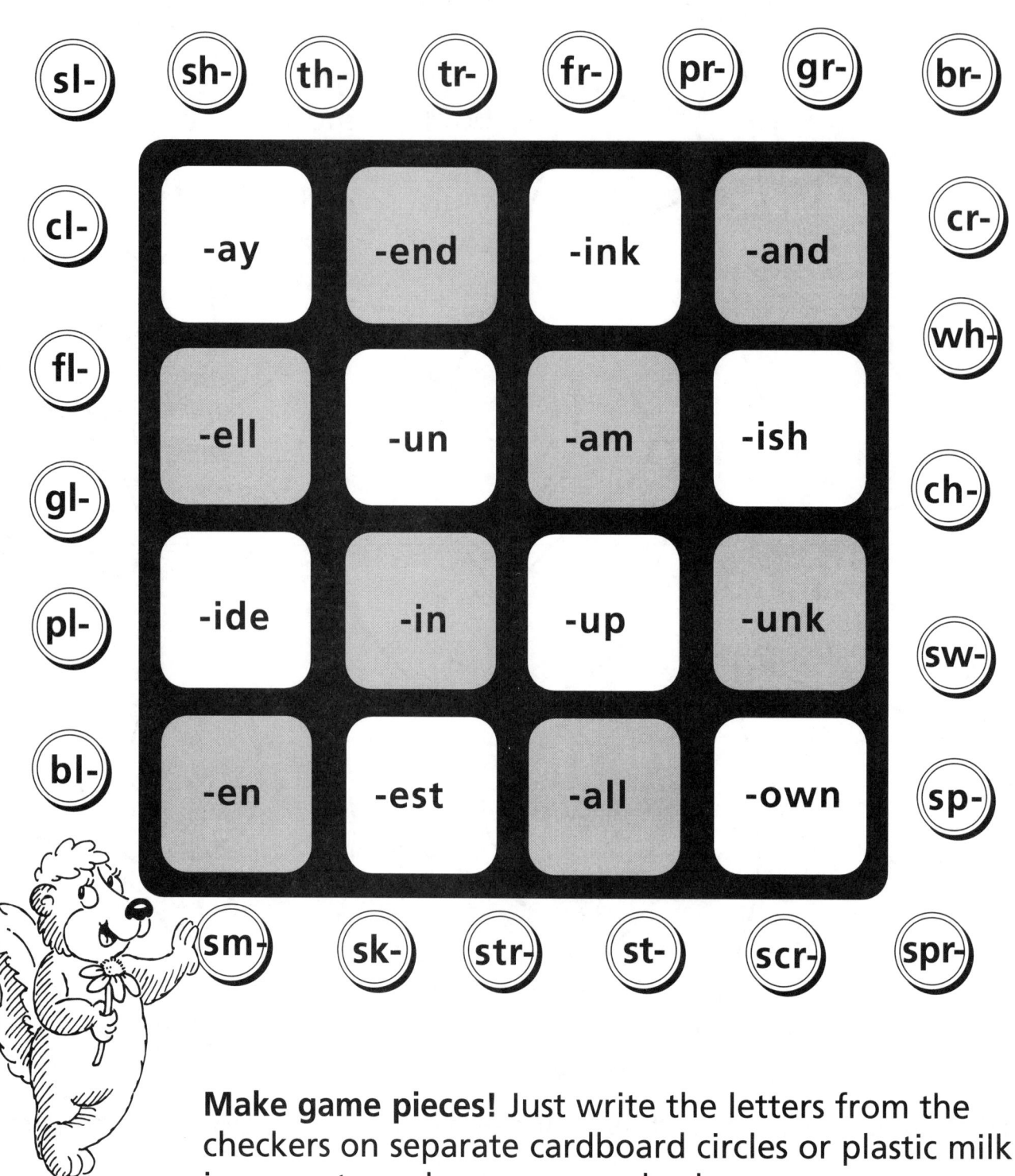

Make game pieces! Just write the letters from the checkers on separate cardboard circles or plastic milk jug caps to make your own checkers.

Super Sundae

Read a book for each category on the super sundae. Color the ice cream scoop for the category when you are finished with the book. When you have read all seven types of books, you will have earned the award at the bottom of the page.

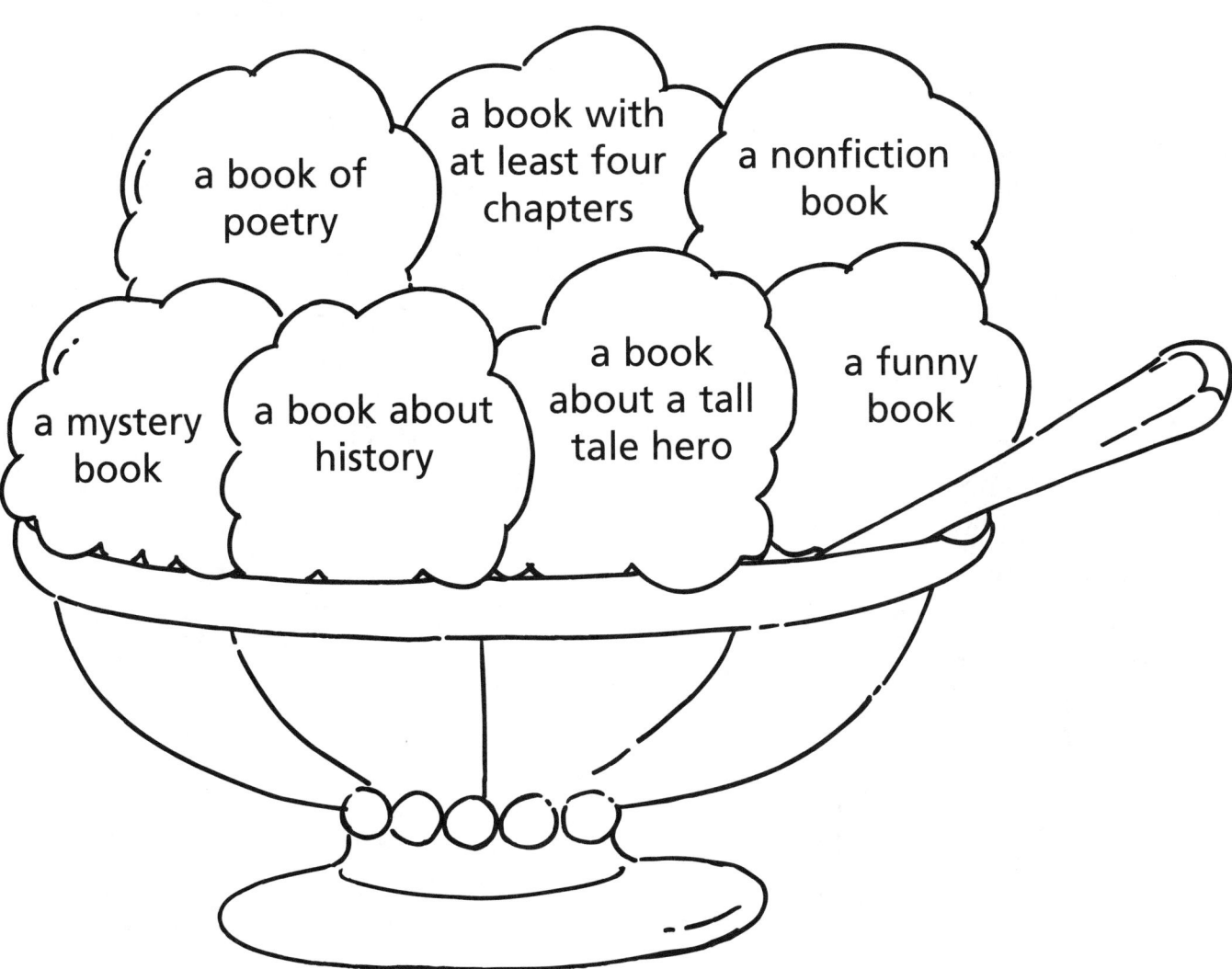

a book of poetry

a book with at least four chapters

a nonfiction book

a mystery book

a book about history

a book about a tall tale hero

a funny book

Congratulations!
The Super Sundae Reading Award
is presented to

_____

You are a reading superstar!

Desert Descriptions

Look at the words in the basket.
Look up unfamiliar words in a dictionary.
Write the nouns on the hump labeled <u>Nouns</u>.
Write the adjectives on the hump labeled <u>Adjectives</u>.

A **noun** is the name of a person, place, or thing.
An **adjective** is a word that describes a noun.

oasis	hot
sandy	cactus
camel	caravan
arid	prickly
desert	tough

Nouns   Adjectives

Challenge! Think of two more nouns and adjectives that match something you are studying at school. Write them on the correct humps.

Get in Gear

Read the word on each gear. On the empty spokes, write other words that have about the same meaning. You may use words from the Synonym Box.

Synonym Box

furious	answered
superb	handsome
asked	excellent
livid	gorgeous

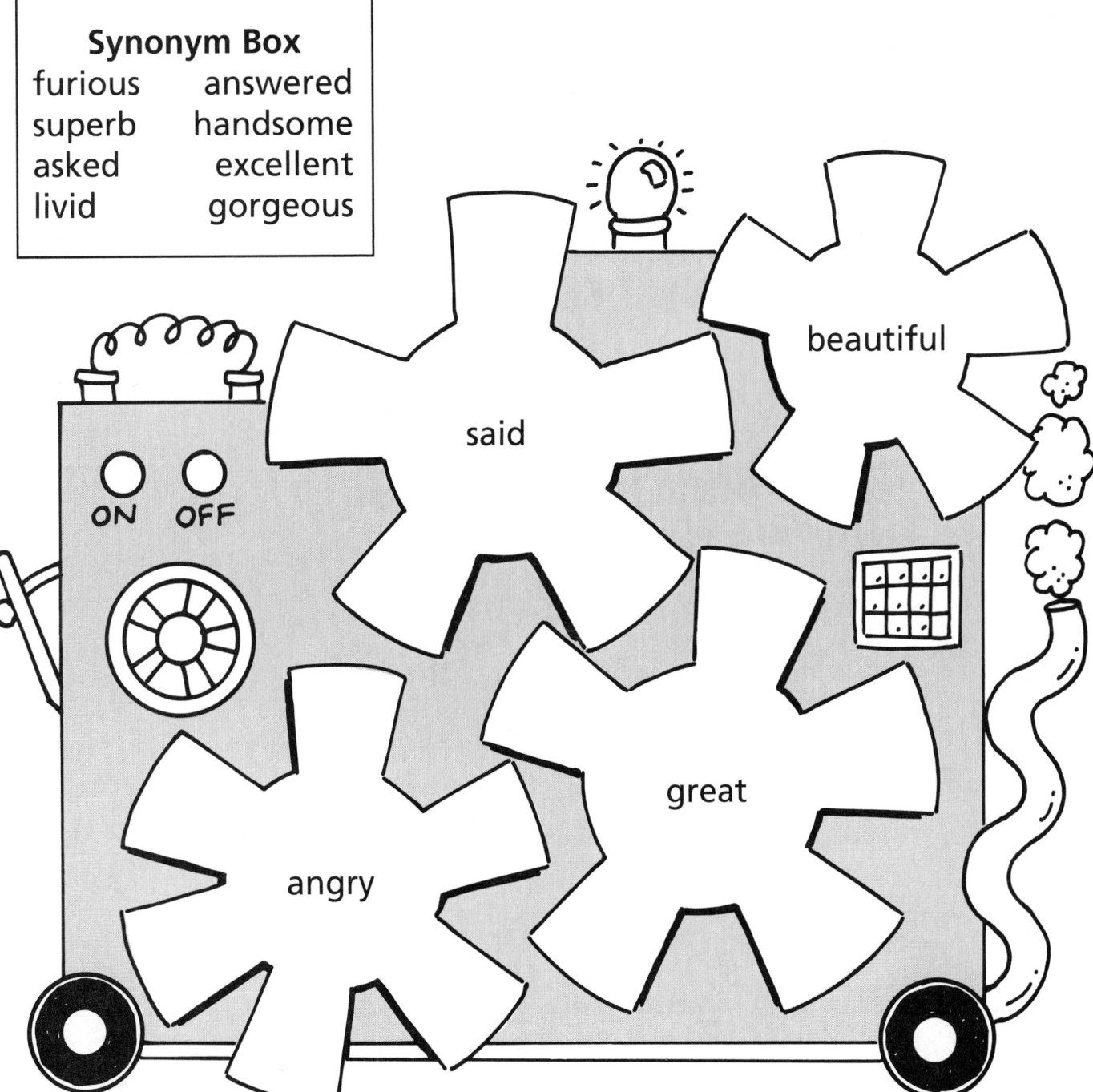

Tip! Remember to use some of these words when you write. Your stories will be more interesting.

Going Bananas!

This monkey only eats complete sentences. Color the bananas next to the sentences it will eat. Rewrite the phrases to make them complete sentences.

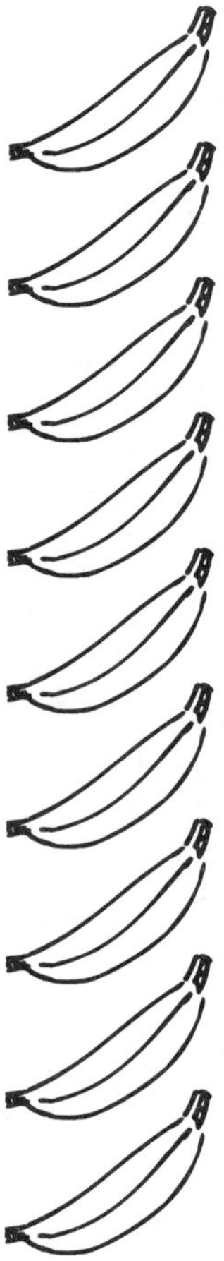

Our class is studying the rain forest.

Live in the rain forest.

Tropical rain forests are found near the equator.

Howler monkeys, spider monkeys, and woolly monkeys.

Howler monkeys are so noisy you can hear them from over two miles away.

Harpy eagles eat monkeys.

Swing from branch to branch.

Mother monkeys carry their young everywhere.

Some monkeys use their tails like arms.

_____

_____

_____

_____

_____

SCOPE Out the Circus

Use the SCOPE method to proofread and edit these sentences. Write each sentence correctly on the line.

S: Check your sentences.
C: Check the capital letters.
O: Check the order.
P: Check the punctuation.
E: EXCELLENT EDITING!

1. jasmine and joe are going to the circus today

_____

2. have you ever been to the circus

_____

3. the circus will travel all over the united states

_____

4. my cousins will see it in alaska

_____

5. tomorrow the boys and girls from oak lane school will go on a field trip

_____

_____

6. they will meet some circus performers

_____

_____

I Spy Number Words

Find and circle these numbers in the puzzle. They may go across, down, or diagonally.

Numbers

eight hundred seventy-six
two hundred three
one hundred fifty-four
three hundred fifty-six
five hundred eighty-five
seven hundred forty
four hundred sixty-two
nine hundred fifty-four
six hundred ninety-six

6	8	7	2	0	3	4	3
0	9	4	5	6	8	2	7
9	5	6	6	1	1	5	4
9	3	2	3	5	6	8	7
4	5	7	8	7	6	5	4
7	8	4	5	4	4	6	0

Now find some of your own and write them!

I found _____

_____

_____

_____

Try these brainteasers! five thousand four hundred forty-six
six thousand ninety-nine
seven thousand five hundred sixteen

Magnificent Measuring

I measured my pencil.

It was about _____ centimeters long.

It was about _____ inches long.

I measured my favorite book.

It was about _____ centimeters high.

It was about _____ inches high.

I measured my toothbrush.

It was about _____ centimeters long.

It was about _____ inches long.

I measured my favorite photograph.

It was about _____ centimeters wide.

It was about _____ inches wide.

I measured my comb.

It was about _____ centimeters long.

It was about _____ inches long.

I measured my smile.

It was about _____ centimeters wide.

It was about _____ inches wide.

inches

centimeters

Subtraction Scoop

Subtract. If a problem was easy enough that you could do it in your head, color its cone brown.

$$\begin{array}{r} 92 \\ -\ 36 \\ \hline \end{array}$$

$$\begin{array}{r} 87 \\ -\ 10 \\ \hline \end{array}$$

$$\begin{array}{r} 48 \\ -\ 36 \\ \hline \end{array}$$

$$\begin{array}{r} 71 \\ -\ 44 \\ \hline \end{array}$$

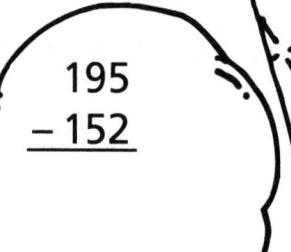
$$\begin{array}{r} 66 \\ -\ 49 \\ \hline \end{array}$$

$$\begin{array}{r} 50 \\ -\ 25 \\ \hline \end{array}$$

$$\begin{array}{r} 100 \\ -\ 20 \\ \hline \end{array}$$

$$\begin{array}{r} 195 \\ -\ 152 \\ \hline \end{array}$$

$$\begin{array}{r} 143 \\ -\ 78 \\ \hline \end{array}$$

$$\begin{array}{r} 942 \\ -\ 42 \\ \hline \end{array}$$

$$\begin{array}{r} 675 \\ -\ 481 \\ \hline \end{array}$$

$$\begin{array}{r} 507 \\ -\ 321 \\ \hline \end{array}$$

Multiplication Drill

Multiply to finish each chart.

x	5	0	3	9	6	2	4	8	7
1									
2				18					
3									

x	3	7	1	8	6	5	9	4
4			4					
5								
6								

x	4	9	0	7	5	3	2	6	8
7									
8						24			

x	2	5	8	3	9	7	4	6
9								
10	20							

A Beginning Budget

Use this budget to plan how you will use your money for one month.

Current Balance (What I have now)

In my savings account: At home: Total:

_____ + _____ = _____

Income (What I will earn or receive this month)

Amount: _____ Reason: _____

Amount: _____ Reason: _____

Amount: _____ Reason: _____

Amount: _____ Reason: _____

Spending (What I would like to do with the money)

Amount: _____ Reason: _____

Amount: _____ Reason: _____

Amount: _____ Reason: _____

Amount: _____ Reason: _____

Melting Matter

Ice is the solid form of water.
Write three ways you can change an ice cube into a liquid.
Circle the method you think will be the fastest.

#1 _____ #2 _____ #3 _____

_____ _____ _____

_____ _____ _____

_____ _____ _____

_____ _____ _____

_____ _____ _____

Work with an adult to test your prediction. Use a stopwatch, kitchen timer, or a clock to time how long it takes to melt an ice cube. Use a different ice cube for each method.

How long did each method take?

#1 _____ #2 _____ #3 _____

Why do you think the fastest method was the fastest?

_____

_____

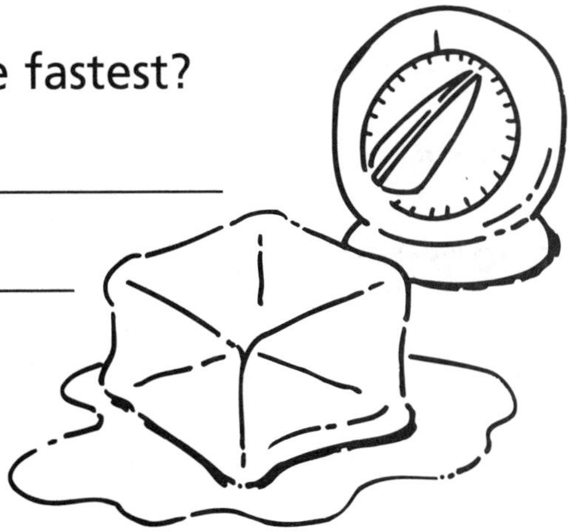

The Water Cycle

Write words from the Word Box to fill in the blanks.

Word Box
cycle
condensation
droplets
evaporation
precipitation
snow
sun
water

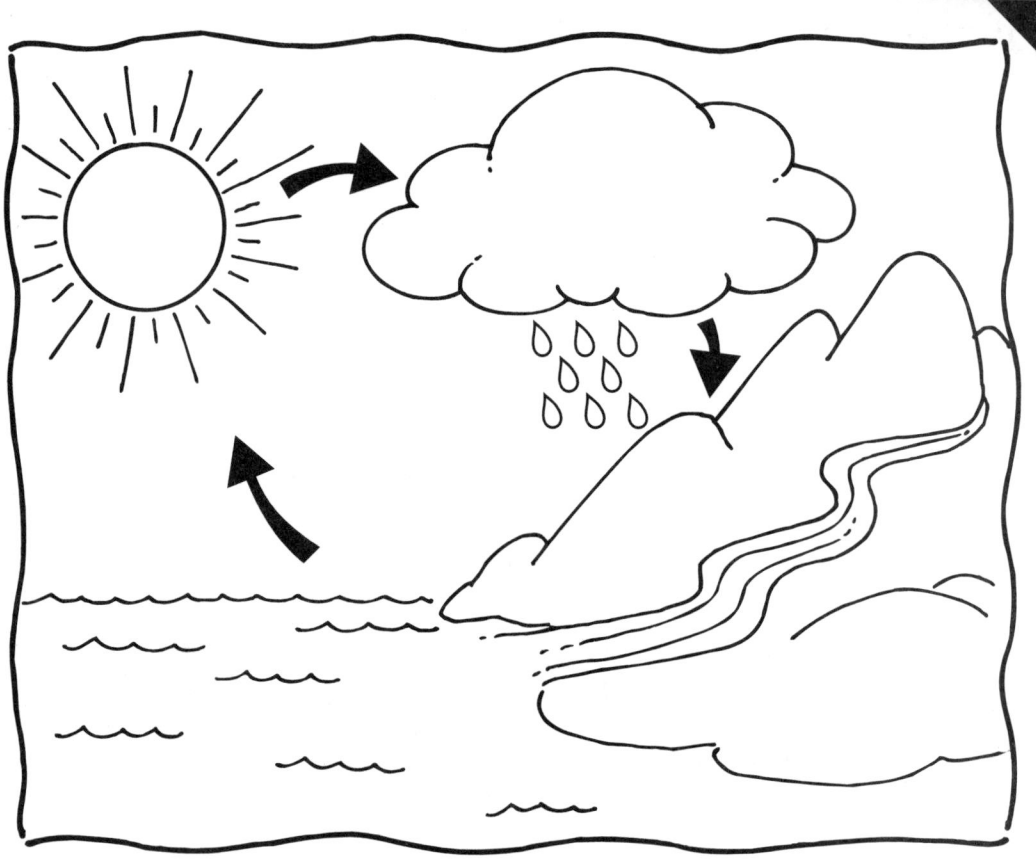

Water moves from the earth into the air and back to the earth over and over again. This is called the water _ _ _ _ _. The _ _ _ heats water in puddles, rivers, and seas. The heated water changes to a gas called _ _ _ _ _ vapor. This change is called _ _ _ _ _ _ _ _ _ _ _. The water vapor rises and moves with the air. High in the sky the air cools. The vapor changes back into water _ _ _ _ _ _ _ _. This is called _ _ _ _ _ _ _ _ _ _ _ _. The droplets form clouds. Water falls from the clouds as rain, hail, sleet, or _ _ _ _. These are all forms of _ _ _ _ _ _ _ _ _ _ _ _ _.

Think Like a Scientist!

Scientists make predictions. They try to guess what the results of an experiment will be before they complete the experiment.

Predict which of the following items you think will float in water. If you think the item will float, draw a happy face beside it. If you think it will sink, draw a sad face. Draw a silly face if you think it will do both.

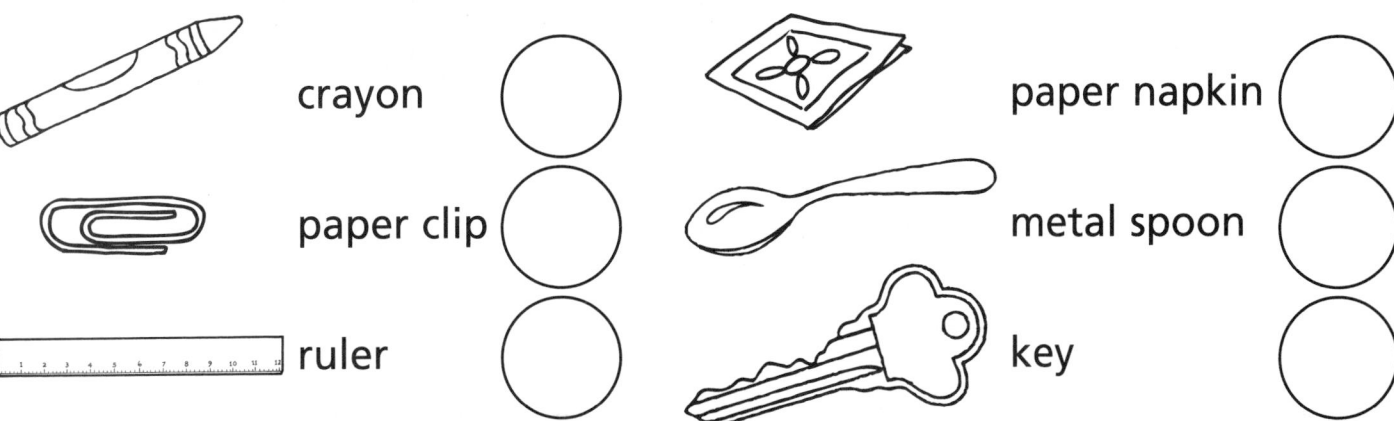

crayon ◯

paper clip ◯

ruler ◯

paper napkin ◯

metal spoon ◯

key ◯

Scientists test their predictions with experiments. Find out how many of your predictions are correct. Fill a sink with water. Place each item above in the water. Watch what happens. Record the results on the chart below.

	Floats	Sinks	Does Both
crayon			
paper clip			
ruler			
paper napkin			
metal spoon			
key			

Hooked on Magnets

What sticks to a magnet?
Find a magnet.
Then do a hunt through your
home to discover the answers.

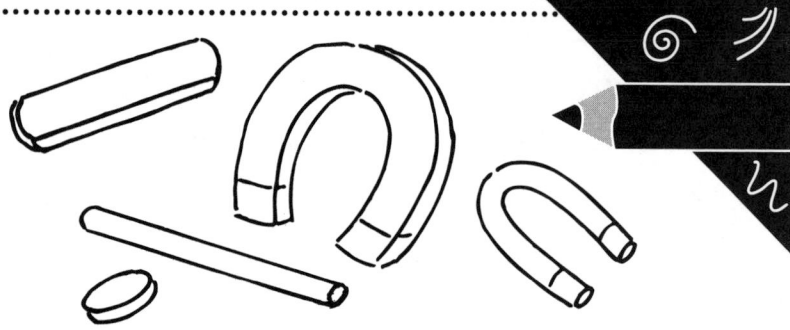

These things **stick**
to a magnet:

_____

_____

_____

_____

_____

_____

_____

These things **do not stick**
to a magnet:

_____

_____

_____

_____

_____

_____

_____

Draw Your Community

Write the street addresses for the following places in your community. Draw a symbol for each place.

Symbol

Your home _____

A friend's home _____

Your school _____

City Hall _____

Post Office _____

Use the grid below to draw a map of your community. Use the symbol for each place above to show where it is located in the community. Label the names of the streets.

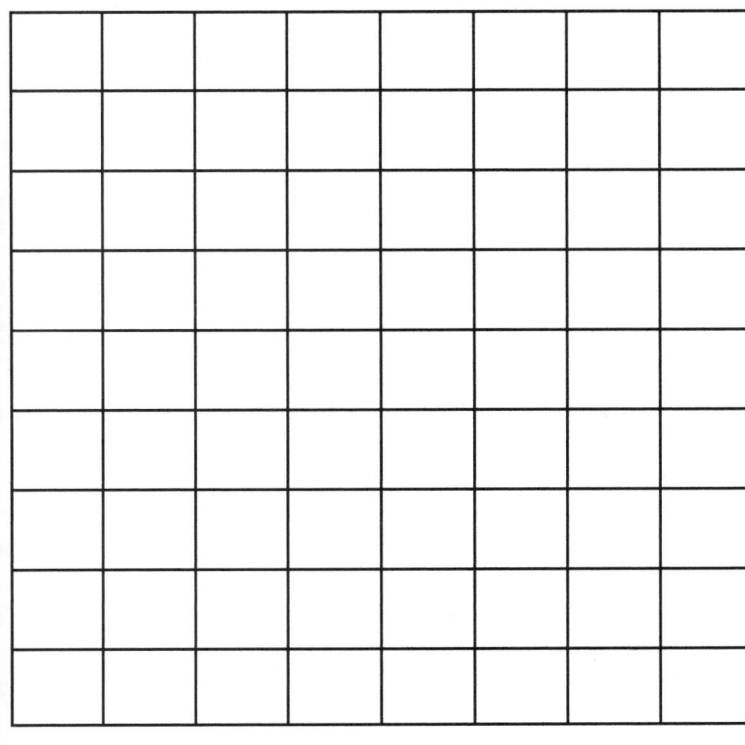

Where Are You?

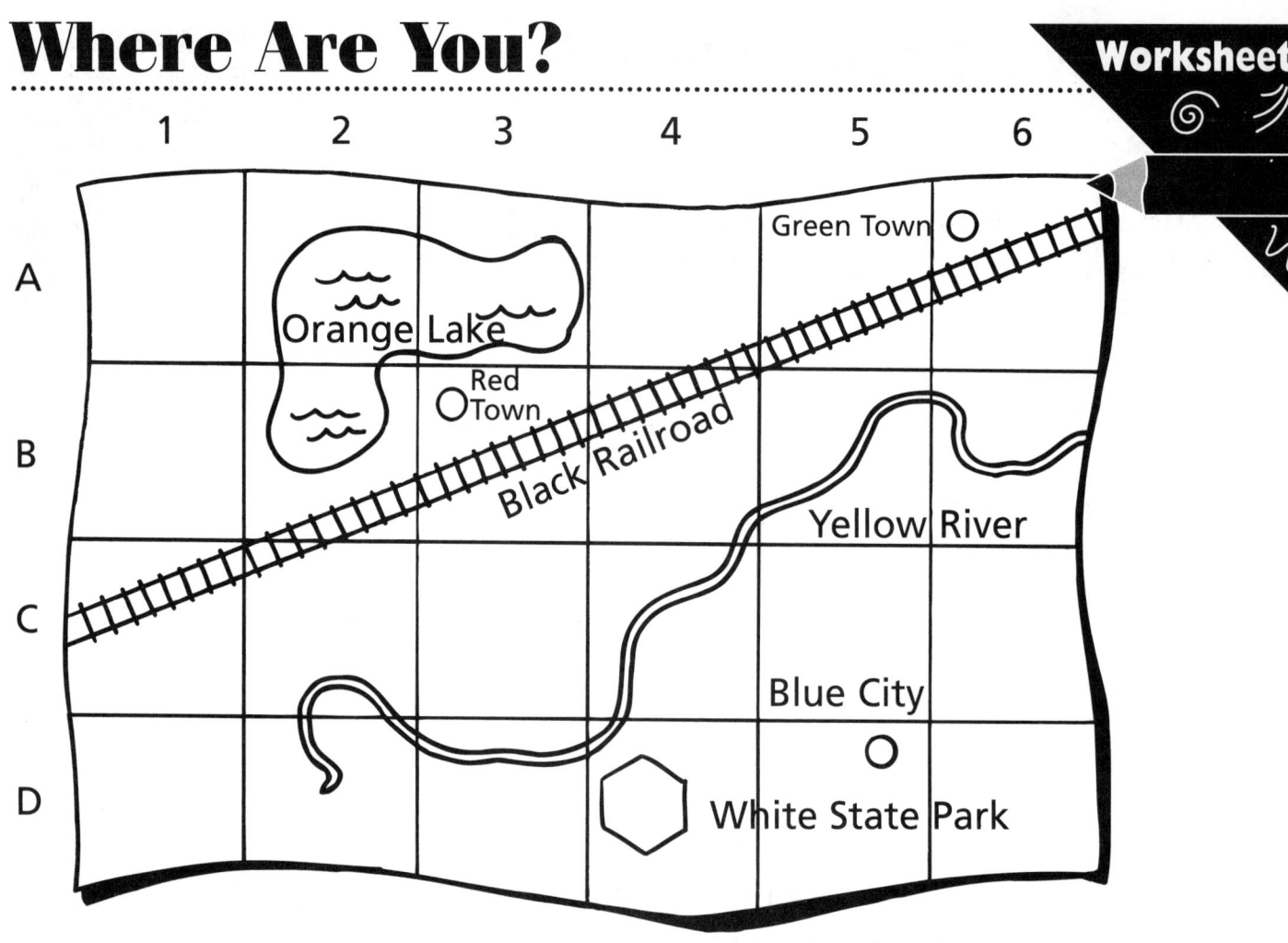

Knowing how to use a map grid can help you find places on a map. Use the map above to complete these items.

1. The Black Railroad runs from C1 to _____.

2. What town is in D5? _____

3. Where would you find Green Town? _____

4. Does the Yellow River flow in B3? _____

5. In which grid boxes is Orange Lake found? _____ _____ _____

6. The Purple Mountains were left off the map by mistake. Draw and label them in C1 and C2.

You Try It! Find a map of your state that uses a grid. Read the map index to learn which grid box your town or city is in. Can you find it on the map?

Graph It!

Keep a record of the number and type of books you read or listen to for a month. Make a bar graph to show the information.

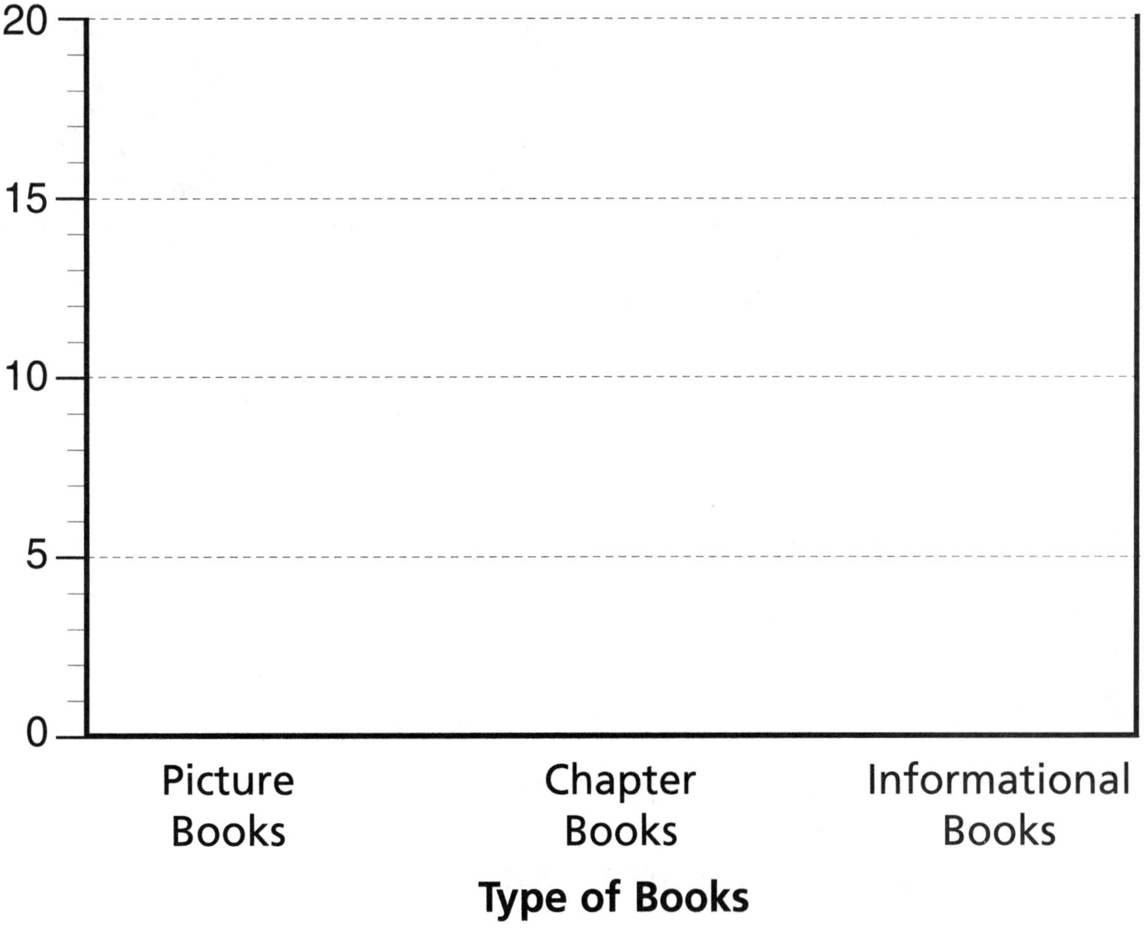

Number of Books

20
15
10
5
0

Picture Books   Chapter Books   Informational Books

Type of Books

1. Which type of book did you read the most? _____

2. Which type of book did you read the least? _____

3. How many chapter books did you read? _____

4. If you wanted to show you had read 13 picture books, where would

   you find 13 on the graph? _____

The History of Me

Follow the steps below to make a time line of your life.

I was born!

A. Answer these questions.

1. What year is it now? _____

2. What year were you born? _____

3. What year did you start school? _____

4. What year did you start to walk? _____

5. What year did you learn to ride a bike? _____

6. In what year was each of your brothers or sisters born?

_____

B. Label the years on the long slanted lines of the time line. Begin with the year you were born. The distance between long lines is two years.

C. Mark important events in your life on the time line. You can use those from Section A if you want.

Proud Clouds

Here are things I can do that I am really proud to tell you about.

nvite everyone in your family to make a "proud clouds" page!

Homework Checklist

Here's what needs to be done for _____.
(date)

Reading _____

☐ It's all finished!

Math _____

☐ It's all finished!

Writing _____

☐ It's all finished!

Science _____

☐ It's all finished!

Social Studies _____

☐ It's all finished!

Other _____

☐ It's all finished!